Ultraviolet
Voices

Stories of Women on the Autism Spectrum

Autism West Midlands • UK

Ultraviolet Voices: Stories of Women on the Autism Spectrum

Copyright © 2014 by Elisabeth Hurley except as otherwise indicated. The copyright to each chapter is owned by the respective author. All rights reserved.

Designed by Sarah Francis

Edited by Elisabeth Hurley

Published by Autism West Midlands

No part of this book may be reproduced in any manner whatsoever without written permission except in the case of brief quotations embodied in critical articles or reviews. For information, address Autism West Midlands, Regent Court, George Road, Edgbaston, Birmingham, B15 1NU

Printed in the United Kingdom

ISBN-13: 978-0-9576541-4-3 (paperback)

Acknowledgment

Autism West Midlands would like to thank the women who participated in the making of this book, as well as their partners and families. We are honoured by your faith in us, and hope this book does your words justice.

Contents

Foreword
Dr Juli Crocombe

Juli is Clinical Director for Autism for St Andrew's, and a Consultant Forensic Psychiatrist in Neurodevelopmental Psychiatry. She has over 15 years experience of working with people with autism who have complex mental health needs and/or offending behaviour. She serves on many external boards and committees, including the NICE Quality Standards Advisory Committee on Autism, the Scientific Advisory Committee of Research Autism and the Editorial Board of the National Autistic Society (NAS) Annual Professional Conference. She was recently elected as Chair of the Advisory Board to the All Party Parliamentary Group on Autism, having been a member of the group for over 10 years.

Juli's research interests include developing our understanding of how to reduce offending behaviour in people with autism. She was the Lead Researcher for a study to establish the prevalence of autism amongst women in Broadmoor Hospital, and is currently engaged in a project to investigate the prevalence of ASD in the prison population.

Juli holds the title of Visiting Teacher within the department of Forensic and Neurodevelopmental Science within the Institute of Psychiatry, a School of King's College, London.

I am delighted to introduce 'Ultraviolet Voices', a book about women on the autism spectrum written by experts – women on the autism spectrum. The personal stories told in these pages are both inspiring and informative, and will prove a great resource for women on the spectrum, their family and friends and all those who seek to understand and support them.

Growing up in the 21st Century is a challenge for all young women, struggling to navigate the uncharted path between traditional 'female' values and expectations and the burgeoning opportunities to compete in what were once 'male' domains. Social rules and values are ever changing in response to the new world of 'social media' and there are now even more opportunities to 'get it wrong' when interacting with others.

For women on the autism spectrum the challenge of 'getting it right' is even greater and sadly, as a Psychiatrist, it is only too often that I meet women on the spectrum who have mental health problems, notably debilitating anxiety and depression, as a result. For some of these women their mental illness has developed because it has not been recognised that they are on the autism spectrum, and they and others are struggling to understand their challenges and needs. Others are recognised as being on the spectrum, but are not provided with the understanding and support that they need to meet these challenges. Regrettably, in far too many cases, their social challenges and resultant vulnerabilities are recognised and taken advantage of by opportunistic individuals who mistreat and abuse them.

Our knowledge and understanding of the autism spectrum continues to grow, not least in that whereas it was once considered to be a primarily 'male' condition we now recognise that there are also women on the spectrum. However, whilst core features are the same in both sexes, the way in which these features are exhibited can be much more subtle in women than in men and, therefore, more difficult to recognise.

The personal stories shared in this book evidence this difficulty in recognition and the resultant failure to understand the challenges and needs of women on the autism spectrum. However, the combined experiences of these inspirational women provides a wealth of information to further grow our knowledge and understanding to enable us to support them in achieving their full potential in life.

Introduction

Historically, autism has been described with a strong male bias. There are more men diagnosed with autism than women (on average four times as many), but it is currently unclear how much of this is due to biological reasons and how much is due to the fact that women with autism are not as well understood and therefore may not be diagnosed.

The aim of this book is to give people a glimpse of autism from a woman's point of view. Every person with autism is different, and this is just as true in women as it is in men. You will find that each woman's story is different and they each have a unique experience of autism. We have a variety of contributions including poetry, artwork and interviews, and our contributors include women who were diagnosed as children, women recently diagnosed, women who are married with children and even one woman who has not yet been diagnosed. We also have contributions from mothers of girls with autism, some of whom are also diagnosed themselves. We are very lucky that some of these young girls have also contributed their own artwork and stories. With the wide variety of contributions, you will see many different ways of putting thoughts into words, lots of different writing styles and lots of ways of expressing emotions!

We are also delighted to have contributions from Dr Wendy Lawson, who writes about autism in women, and ageing, and Robyn Steward, a woman with autism who talks about understanding abuse. Robyn is very frank about abuse and it is worth noting that some of the content of her chapter may not be suitable for younger or sensitive readers. It is, however, an extremely valuable chapter which I would encourage all women, particularly those with autism, to read and to take on board its messages.

We end the book with a chapter focussing on the current understanding of autism in women and girls. This chapter aims to develop your knowledge of the research in this area and highlight differences between men and women with autism.

Please note that for privacy reasons, some names in the book have been changed. If this has been done, a replacement name will be used and there will be a star (*) next to it the first time it is used.

We would like to thank all of the contributors for their valuable work. We hope that you enjoy the book and find it a rewarding and entertaining read.

Chapter 1
Victoria Mason

Victoria Mason is 31 and was diagnosed with Asperger Syndrome in 2013. Her diagnosis has given her a new insight into her life and helped her to see events in her life more clearly.

Part One
Asperger's: An Analogy

Life is a game of tennis, the world a tennis court, its citizens tennis players. People simply learn the rules and join in the game. During the game, information passes back and forth, from player to player. Each player has a tool with which they receive and send this information. This tool is a tennis racket.

Well, most players have a tennis racket. I don't. I have a badminton racket. Now, tennis rackets and badminton rackets do have some similarities; they share many of the same properties and functions, and can, from a distance, be mistaken.

Many other players in the game don't even realise I'm holding a badminton racket. I look the part in my tennis whites and trainers, my hair tied in a sporty pony-tail and carrying my stylish tennis racket case. Tennis rackets themselves come in such a variety of shapes and sizes nowadays anyway: new materials, go-faster stripes, super lightweight, extendable, retractable, never breakable. I have made my badminton racket look as much like a tennis racket as possible: new handle, new strings and a bit of stretching and pulling and bending, although it's still a badminton racket underneath.

Some aspects of a tennis game don't require a racket at all: physical strength, nutrition, movement around the court, knowing the rules. I have learned how to play to my strengths and get the most from my badminton racket. It takes extra practice, focus, determination and a bit more time than if I had a tennis racket, but it is not impossible. With my badminton racket I have developed my own, unique style of tennis.

I can learn the rules of the game as well as anybody else. In fact, a bit better than most, because I know I need every advantage I can get. So, I've learned the rules, the history, and the theory behind the game. Although it doesn't come naturally, I know what I'm meant to do and what other people are doing. I've watched what everybody else does and I copy it as best I can. Some parts of the game I can participate in just as well as everybody else, I enjoy myself even, and forget about my disguised badminton racket. I can't avoid hitting the ball forever though.

Depending on my opponents, partners and the nature of the game I can do well at times. Some players are patient and tolerant. Others have been injured or have broken strings or are preoccupied so don't notice my mistakes. Sooner or later, however, the truth comes out: my badminton racket just doesn't send or receive the ball in the same way as other people's tennis rackets.

Then it all gets a bit difficult. Some people can't see that there is a problem. "You're young, fit and intelligent", they say, "just do what everybody else does. You'll get the hang of it." They get frustrated at me and think I'm not trying hard enough or am deliberately missing the ball.

Occasionally I feel too embarrassed or too tired to explain what is different. Playing tennis with a badminton racket can be truly exhausting. So, I avoid playing, or slope off for some time-out to recover. I go and sit high up in the bleachers, away from the limitations of the court. That's not quite my world, not quite designed for the imposter badminton racket.

Sometimes, people can be unkind. They perceive that I am different so they exclude me from their team. They can be worried that my racket won't return the ball in the nice, usual, predictable way they expect. I may hit outside of the lines. Some people are embarrassed by me.

Every now and then, I try to explain what the problem is. I explain how my racket reacts in a different way. People think I'm making excuses. "We all have bad days sometimes," they try to be reassuring. "You have to take the losing with the winning," they smile. "Why don't you try a bit harder?" Some people tell me how they have overcome problems with their tennis rackets, they replaced old strings and suddenly the ball flew about the court, or they changed the angle of the ball toss and suddenly increased the power of their serve. They are so well-meaning that it seems ungrateful for me to keep saying that they've not quite understood.

And so the game continues, the balls flying back and forth, gaining speed, gaining momentum, gaining strength. I join in the best I can. Most people assume I have a tennis racket just like they do. Many people only play with or against me for a short while every now and again and I have learned enough compensatory skills to fool most people for this short time. It's only during prolonged, intense matches that others notice something different.

Sometimes how I yearn for a tennis racket! Just to be able to join in without shame, embarrassment or guilt; to experience what other people seem to experience so easily, to feel how other people feel. I can't help but think that life would be so much easier.

Other times I'm grateful for my badminton racket. Occasionally I've been able to perform the most unique shots and win some unexpected points. Part of me quite likes being different. Even with my unusual racket there are times when I have experienced the success of making a perfect shot, the excitement of winning a tough point or the joy of teaching a younger player how to hit the ball. I can see how it can be a truly fascinating game and often I want to be part of it.

My one wish would be to have a tennis racket just for a day. One day so that I could compare the two and find out what, if anything, I am missing. Although I can imagine how it must feel to hold a tennis racket, I don't actually know how it feels. I'd like to know. I'd like the tennis racket-wielding folk to know how it feels to play with a badminton racket too.

Here, the referees have been trained in the ways of tennis and enforcing these rules and traditions brings a feeling of safety and security. The coaches know only how to coach tennis, and bring up the next generation of tennis players. The spectators are informed and knowledgeable about tennis. You need to play tennis matches to get somewhere in the tennis world.

Navigating the tennis world gets a bit easier over time, as I'm sure it does for those with tennis rackets too. At least everything makes a bit more sense now I know I have a badminton racket. I used to think I had a tennis racket, just the same as everybody else, and got frustrated and depressed that I couldn't use it properly, no matter how hard I tried. I wasn't sure what I was doing wrong.

So, I walk onto court, clutching my racket bag, sipping my drink, ready for the next match. I look around and take in the atmosphere. I am fed up of pretending; it is exhausting and I never reach my potential.

I walk to the service line and begin my warm up. If only life were the Olympic Games, the world a multi-sports arena and its citizens a range of athletes. On a badminton court, with a shuttle and undisguised racket, with badminton coaches and a supportive environment, I could improve and learn without shame or guilt. I could be quite happy just being me.

Part Two
Asperger's and me

Asperger's has always been a part of me, although it wasn't until my late twenties that I knew this word described my set of differences and abilities. The best way I can find of describing what it is like to live with Asperger's is the tennis analogy above. Something inside me processes information (sensory, social and emotional information) and interprets the world in a different way to the way the majority of other people seem to process the same information.

Here, in such short a space, it is impossible for me to describe all of the events, emotions and experiences that make me who I am, and I can't possibly begin to give you the complete picture of all the ways in which Asperger's affects my life. What I can do, however, is attempt to give you some insight into where I fit along the autistic spectrum.

But you can't have Asperger's. You're nothing like the characters from The Big Bang Theory. You have social skills.

Hmmm, that programme has a lot to answer for! You're right; I don't stand out as being obviously socially inappropriate or awkward. The difference is that I have had to learn these skills. Through experience, observation, copying, some explicit teaching, and lots of reading I have learned the mechanics of social skills. I understand what suitable topics of conversation are, can do small-talk, and use appropriate facial expression and body language. I no longer feel as awkward and as out of place in social situations as I used to, as I know that I have these skills and can appear as skilled as the average person.

My differences are less obvious and probably only noticeable once I get to know people. I love presenting to groups and can enjoy one-to-one conversations. Taking part in a group conversation, however, is a different story. I find it difficult to know when I can speak and what I should say. I often seem to interrupt people without intending to. I often seem to say things that stop the flow of the conversation, even though I don't intend to do that either! If something of interest is brought up in discussion, my thoughts will go off in different directions. By the time I've thought through my point of view or my response, the other speakers are often discussing something else, making it seem like I've not listened to their next comment, or that I'm fixating on something.

I have been told that other people can think I'm bringing up the same topic over and over again. Other people don't seem to do this. They have a conversation and then go on to something else, or totally forget about it. I'll often want to discuss the same thing several times, maybe a day or a week after the original conversation. I don't think I'm being repetitive or boring, it's just that my thinking is evolving and every time I come back to something it's because I have something to add, or want to consider something from a different perspective. By this time, other people have long since forgotten the original conversation and have lost interest in the subject!

But you seem quite normal. Aren't all people with Asperger's just interested in quantum physics/trains/video games?

I have similar interests to a lot of women; I think the difference has always been the intensity of my interests. When I was eleven years old, for example, I developed an interest in Coronation Street. Now, it is quite typical to enjoy soap operas, and I knew that it was perfectly okay for me to ask my classmates if they had watched the previous evening's episode. I knew it wasn't perfectly okay for me to tell them how many bricks the Rovers Return was made out of or the exact dates each character had made their first appearance, how I was making a scale model of the set, how I taped every episode and re-watched the scenes containing my favourite characters, or how I knew every fact there was to know about the programme.

This is typical of all of my hobbies and interests. When I become interested in something, it can take over my life and make everything else seem supremely unimportant. Life always seems more interesting when I have an interest. My intense interests have included German grammar, Agatha Christie books, triathlon, the history of the Olympic Games, linguistics, The Sound of Music, education and many, many other things. I simply cannot understand how somebody who says they are interested in something could not want to find out absolutely everything about that thing in as short a time as possible! Luckily this focus to learn things has worked very well for me, as some of my later interests were related to specific school subjects and work-related issues, meaning that I gained skills and knowledge useful for study and employment.

Incidentally, my interests can change very quickly and I lose interest as quickly as I gain interest. At the age of eleven, I based my life around watching Coronation Street; now I hate watching television, especially soap operas, and can't understand in the slightest what it was that fascinated me so much!

And what about sensory issues? Aren't they part of Asperger's?

Yes, they can be. I do have some sensory differences and can feel overloaded by too much sensory information. Bright, artificial lights aren't good; neither is lots of noise, especially not different noises at once. Trying to have a conversation when other people are talking nearby and the television is on is almost impossible! Feeling uncomfortable in certain clothing can also be an issue – I couldn't wear jeans, or anything that didn't have an elasticated waist, until I was in my early 20s because of the 'feel' of the material. Touch can be an issue. There are certain things that I just can't touch (other people's food and Tupperware, for example) and I can't stand being in crowds of people or in rooms with no windows.

It sounds quite normal not to like bright lights, loud noises or crowds of people. How do you feel 'overloaded'?

This is very difficult to explain! Let me try to give you some examples. Okay, so first take a supermarket - this is one of my least favourite environments - there are very bright strip lights and no windows or natural light. Everything is shiny and there are so many products; the whole place is visually overwhelming. Then there is the noise: the in-store music, the announcements, babies crying, people talking and laughing, the hum of the lights and fridges, the check-outs beeping and trolleys squeaking. There are crowds of people invading my personal space, leaning over to get their groceries, people stopping in front of me, children running around, people moving in different directions, people standing too close to me in the queue. All of these things begin to overwhelm me and I feel anxious and uncomfortable. To cope with this, my body begins to shut down. I try to shut out the noise, I put my hand above my eyes to shut out some of the 'glare' and I block out everything that is going on. I feel physically uncomfortable so do things like tie my hair up or remove my jacket. I am concentrating so much on 'surviving' that I can become oblivious to others, not noticing when people are talking to me and becoming slower than usual in responding. Trying to block out my surroundings takes all of my energy, so I forget what groceries I need, I can't focus on making a decision about what to buy for dinner and I become confused. If I get to this point I usually have to leave my trolley and walk out of the supermarket to recover. For me, recovery from sensory over-stimulation requires a complete lack of stimulation. Lying down in a dark, empty, absolutely silent room in my most comfortable clothes is absolutely perfect!

Another example is in social situations. Imagine chatting to some friends in a room full of other people, all having their own conversations. I find it extremely difficult to filter out this background noise. It always seems louder to me than it does to other people, so all of my energy is taken up on blocking this out and trying to focus on my conversation. As a result of this intense blocking out, I find I can't concentrate on the conversation and my responses are delayed as my attention is elsewhere. Non-essentials such as social niceties and appearing relaxed get forgotten. Situations like this can be immensely tiring and exhausting, usually resulting in me becoming very quiet and withdrawn.

Is it not difficult to cope in everyday life?

Well, for me, it is much easier to cope as an independent adult than it was as an undiagnosed child. I know which environments I will find difficult, and I can avoid them. At home, I can arrange my environment so that I feel comfortable. With friends or colleagues, I can ask to move somewhere quieter or to dim the lights. I have control over which clothes I wear and what I do. These things were much more difficult as a child. I couldn't articulate at the time what it was about supermarkets, for example, that made me feel so uncomfortable. As a result, people could think I was being lazy or selfish by not wanting to help with the shopping. My family's idea of a nice evening, sitting and chatting noisily in a very brightly-lit living room with the television on, was my idea of hell!

You don't seem to have any problems with communicating. Aren't people with Asperger's meant to take everything literally?

I don't take language literally. If you tell me that 'it's raining cats and dogs' or that you have a 'bee in your bonnet', I won't expect furry animals to fall suddenly from the sky, nor will I wonder why you haven't removed the offending creature from your hat. I have no trouble understanding metaphorical or idiomatic language. I enjoy reading and studied linguistics at university so have no difficulties with those things. If somebody tells me they will call back in an hour's time, I understand that it might not be in exactly one hour, it may be ten minutes or so either side.

Yet, in some ways I do take things literally. If somebody tells me something, then I assume that they mean what they say. I also remember everything that people tell me. In combination, these two things can cause some difficulties and can sometimes be mistaken for facetiousness.

Difficulties sometimes arise from differences in perception. Think back to my earlier example of my Coronation Street obsession when I was young. Classmates at school would say they also liked the programme. I would then discover this meant they watched it sometimes; they weren't interested in finding out everything about it as I was. To me, this came across as them lying. They weren't, it was just different interpretations of the word 'like'.

A big part of this relates to concepts of truth and honesty. I don't understand 'fakeness' and manipulation. If, for example, I hear people talking negatively about another person, then later I see those same people being nice to that person, it makes me very uncomfortable. I don't know what is real or what to believe. Does this mean that people who are nice to my face don't really like me either? How do I know if somebody likes me or if they are just being pleasant and polite? The social world is very confusing!

There are many instances like this that can cause a lot of confusion in everyday life. I would much rather know the truth, because the truth can't be argued with. For example, I would much rather people told me exactly what they think of me. I might not like what they have to say but at least then I don't have to guess and worry about what they might be thinking! I know that other people have told me they would hate the idea of everybody being honest all of the time, whereas I would feel much more comfortable!

So, can it be difficult interacting with other people?

Yes and no! I can enjoy some social events, but I am not overly sociable and quite enjoy my own company. The difference seems to be something that happens inside me. I don't seem to make the same sort of emotional connection to others. Take, for example, a week away with other people. Whether Brownie camp at age eight, school exchange trips as a teenager, or holidays as an adult – the same thing has always happened to me. Physically I am as present as everybody else. I do the same things, take part in the same conversations, and share the same experiences. At the end of the week, everybody else has made some sort of emotional bond or connection; they have become friends. I haven't. I still feel different and as if I don't belong. Something that seems to happen so easily for other people does not seem to happen in my brain. I used to think I simply needed to try harder, improve my social skills, throw myself into things. That doesn't change things though. It is a sort of emotional invisibility.

Don't people with Asperger's lack feelings, empathy and theory of mind?

I definitely have just as many feelings as everybody else; I just seem to express them in a different way. Let me give you a few examples.

Firstly, it seems to take me a long time to process my emotions. I often don't know how I am feeling until I have had time to think about it! This emotional processing time can mean I have a delayed response to events, and consequently other people may think I am not experiencing any emotions. This can also cause problems with others. "Well, why didn't you just tell me how you were feeling at the time?"

The fact that I need so much emotional processing time can mean I get very frustrated with others. Some people love to tell me what I should be feeling, "Oh, you must be feeling so xyz", "I felt xyz too when that happened to me". That is very frustrating, because most of the time I'm not feeling x, y and z; I would have described my feelings very differently! Then I feel worried because I feel that I'm not feeling the 'right' thing! An example from my childhood was going away on Brownie camp at aged eight: as I excitedly jumped on the bus, the other girls cried and hugged their parents. My parents were furious that I hadn't done the same. "But I was excited about going away. Do you mean I should just pretend to be sad to leave you, even though I'm not?" This made it worse! I just couldn't understand it. My logic was that if the other girls were so sad to be going away, why didn't they just stay at home? It was the first of many times I have been told that I have been feeling the 'wrong' thing. That's the hardest bit about Asperger's. I can pretend to 'do' things, but I can't pretend to 'feel' things that I don't feel.

Sometimes I can appear quite secretive. It can be easier to keep my thoughts, feelings and plans to myself as it feels safer that way. Often, the moment I tell people, they put their own beliefs and values on it and turn it into something different. This, in turn, can make me feel misunderstood.

Next, imagine I am sad or upset. The last thing that I would want is other people around me, hugging me and talking to me. I dislike sympathy and pity. If I am dealing with my emotions, the very last thing I can do is deal with other people at the same time! So, something that I can consider selfless (not inflicting my distress on other people), can come across as being selfish to others ("why won't you let us help you?").

I can definitely feel empathy for other people; I perhaps just express it more discreetly than others. It can be easy to assume everybody is like us; I therefore assume that other people also do not like a fuss or wouldn't like somebody else telling them how to feel. As I have become older, a greater awareness of my own emotions has helped me to become more capable of expressing empathy towards others.

And, you mentioned theory of mind? I think I would argue that people without autism find it just as difficult to understand those with autism as the other way round!

What about control and inflexibility of thought?

Yes, some people can think that I am being controlling at times; usually this is a type of self-preservation. Controlling my physical environment, for example, is a way of me reducing sensory issues that could lead to melt-down. I find that I have become very well-organised, a 'planner' and very efficient. These are positive skills, especially when in employment or studying. These things have other purposes for me though too. Organisation and planning makes me feel in control and comfortable. I can try to predict and eliminate any situations that may make me feel anxious – I need the preparation to perform at my best as I won't think of things on the spot. I often rehearse situations and events in my head to help me feel prepared. This can be both positive and negative. Sometimes I have prepared for something so much that if something then changes, it can throw me more than if I hadn't prepared at all (i.e. there is a bigger difference between what I have expected and what actually happens). Real life can also be a disappointment if I have rehearsed the perfect scenario in my head so many times. So, sometimes, spontaneity isn't a problem at all. In fact, thinking about it, the times I have felt happiest and most relaxed have probably been spontaneous events.

A lot of things only really become a problem when working with other people. If given a team task in a school or work environment, for example, my initial reaction would always be to go and research and prepare it immediately. This allows me to feel prepared enough to contribute because I need 'thinking space' to be productive. When the team next meets, it can appear to other people that I am trying to 'take over' or even show them up, which isn't the case at all.

When I left school I took a gap year and worked in Germany. Although a totally new and different environment, I looked forward to it enormously. This was because I could read many books for tourists and visitors to Germany, giving a detailed explanation of German customs, traditions, social expectations and language to use. Perfect! Knowing the 'rules' and what was expected made me feel fine.

What else makes up your Asperger's?

Lots of things, far too many to mention in detail! One thing I feel is important is a lack of self-identity. When I was growing up, everybody around me seemed to experience and interpret the world differently. I can recall hundreds of examples of me realising that other people just didn't see things the way that I did. I didn't see myself reflected back in anybody else (real or in the media). I felt that there must be something wrong with me. People told me I wasn't normal or just needed to try harder to fit in. It seemed that because other people were in the majority, they must be 'right'. Thinking like this can, in turn, lead to a whole host of other problems such as depression, worry, anxiety and a lack of self-esteem and confidence.

What's the most important thing you wish people understood?

How important fairness and equality is to me. I like the rulebook to be followed and can't understand how rules can sometimes be broken. This is probably the most difficult aspect of my Asperger's as an adult (and was very important as a child too). I think everything should be open, honest and transparent because I really, really don't understand why it shouldn't be. This can cause particular difficulties in school or work environments – I can't understand why people don't do things they should and just don't get office politics. This can be really difficult because bringing issues up can make others think I'm pernickety, pedantic or a trouble-maker. However, if I don't bring them up, the feelings don't go away and cause me a huge amount of distress. I like having things written down clearly and don't see the point of having policies, programmes or documents if they are meaningless.

Is having Asperger's a problem?

Not now, no. It certainly used to be and I struggled as a teenager and in my twenties because of the reasons mentioned above, and a lot more. I would say for me at least that Asperger's itself isn't the biggest problem – the anxiety, stress and depression it can lead to is the bigger problem.

Realising that I had Asperger's was the most significant moment of my life. Suddenly I realised that I wasn't just odd or not trying hard enough, but that there were hundreds more women out there just like me. I found other people who understood me. Thinking back over my life suddenly everything made a whole lot more sense! I compare it to reading a book in which you discover on the last page that the narrator was the murderer. You then immediately have to go back and re-read the book, every sentence and every event now takes on a different meaning. I had to re-frame my life in light of Asperger's and it turned from a huge tangled ball of knitting wool into a neatly knitted scarf. I could see patterns and reasons, cause and effect and could identify why differences had become difficulties.

For me, Asperger's isn't an illness, a disease or a disorder. It is merely a different way of interpreting the world to the majority of people. In an ideal world, we wouldn't even need a name for it; neuro-diversity would simply be accepted and celebrated. I am, in fact, not sure if I like the idea of being 'labelled'. I had to think carefully about having a formal diagnosis. After all, I am a functioning, coping individual. I am healthy, live independently and responsibly, work full-time and have hobbies, interests and friends. I didn't need a diagnosis, as many people do, for access to services or support. What having a label did do, however, was enable me to become more self-aware and explore what makes me who I am. This in itself was life-changing and was something that I wish had happened when I was a teenager. In fact, for me, realising 'officially' that I was different made me, for the very first time in my life, feel extremely normal indeed.

Chapter 2
Cynthia Kim

Cynthia is the proud owner of many labels including woman, wife, mother, writer, editor, entrepreneur and most recently, autistic. Diagnosed with Asperger syndrome in her early forties, she began blogging about life on the spectrum at musingsofanaspie.com. She is the author of two books, "Nerdy, Shy and Socially Inappropriate: A User Guide to an Asperger Life" and "I Think I Might Be Autistic: A Guide to Autism Spectrum Disorder Diagnosis and Self-Discovery for Adults." When she isn't writing, she can often be found running or hiking backwoods trails somewhere on the East coast of the US.

At five, I wanted to be a boy. I don't know what I thought being a boy meant. Maybe I thought it meant playing outside in the summer, shirtless and barefoot. Maybe I thought it meant not wearing dresses.

Dresses were all scratchy lace trim and tight elastic sleeves. Stiff patent leather shoes pinched my sensitive feet. Perfume tickled my nose. Tights made my legs itch and had maddening seams at the toes. Too young to understand sensory sensitivities, I followed my instincts. While other girls favoured frilly clothes, I gravitated toward the soft comfort of cotton shirts and worn corduroys. Somehow, comfort got mixed up with gender in my head. For decades, "dressing like a girl" meant being uncomfortable. And so began a lifelong tension between being female and being autistic.

*

For a lengthy stretch of adulthood, I had an entire section of my closet that could best be described as aspirational. Pantsuits. Dressy blouses. Pumps and sandals. Skirts, bought and worn once for a special occasion. Dresses, bought and worn never, before being spirited off to the thrift store.

I preferred ripped jeans and running shoes, hoodies and baggy t-shirts. Comfortable and comforting, just as they had been in childhood.

It wasn't until after being diagnosed with Asperger syndrome at the age of forty-two that I learned about sensory sensitivities. Suddenly my aversion to dressy clothes, perfume and make-up made sense. A huge weight lifted. I'd spent decades wondering about my lack of femininity. Where other women revelled in dressing up, I saw only itchy skin and painfully tight seams. Instead of making me feel glamorous, lipstick and eyeliner left me counting the minutes until I could wash my face.

Lacking the explanation that sensory sensitivities eventually provided, I spent decades feeling like I wasn't a "real" woman.

Today I have four dresses hanging in my closet. Made of soft cottons and knits, they're as comfortable as my worn hoodies and jeans. They're not aspirational like my dresses of the past. I wear them when my husband takes me out on date nights. No make-up. No nylons. No tight pinching shoes. I've found a style that suits me, that makes me feel both beautiful and comfortable.

I've learned how to shop in a way that accommodates my sensory needs and I've learned that there is more than one way to be feminine.

*

There are many things I've had to learn or relearn since my diagnosis. Mostly I've had to learn how to be autistic. That sounds like an odd thing to say, after all, I've been autistic all my life. But being autistic and knowing that I'm autistic are two vastly different things.

Knowing that I'm autistic has helped me to reconcile so many confusing aspects of my life. It's as if I'm slowly reassembling the pieces of myself.

There are few role models for autistic women. There is no Rain Woman, no popular stereotype that comes to mind when you hear the phrase autistic woman. Perhaps that's for the better: stereotypes carry with them the burden of proving them wrong.

Still, we face hurdles when it comes to public perceptions of autistic adults. Again and again in my blog's search terms I come across people searching for an answer to questions that surprise me.

Can aspie women marry? Can women with Asperger's have children? Do aspies say "I love you"?

It seems we're a mystery.

I hope that when people find my blog, they see that the answers to all of those things are 'yes'. I'm married. I have a child. I tell my husband and daughter that I love them.

Sadly, that wasn't always the case.

*

Women are expected to be intuitively skilled at social interaction; we are the nurturers, the carers. To be born without natural social instincts can leave you questioning your innate womanhood.

The first hint of what was to come arrived long before I'd given any thought to what being a woman would mean. At some point in sixth grade (when I was about 11), many of the girls in my class became huggers. They hugged when they met each other and when they said goodbye. They hugged when they passed in the hallway. They hugged when they were happy or sad. They hugged and cried and squealed with excitement and I watched from a distance, perplexed. What did all this hugging mean? And more importantly, why wasn't I suddenly feeling the need to hug someone every thirty seconds?

This was the first of many confusing conversations I was to have with myself.

I was a mother and wife for twenty-four years before I was diagnosed with Asperger syndrome. Over and over during that time, I questioned not only my womanhood, but my humanity. I questioned why I didn't respond the way other women did to their children. I watched the other mothers tear up as the bus pulled away on the first day of kindergarten and felt guilty at my relief. *"Finally, a few hours alone"*, was all that was running through my head.

Looking back, I bet the other mums walked back to their newly quiet homes and felt a similar relief. The thing is, I never knew for sure because I didn't talk with any of them. Beyond a friendly "good morning" at the bus stop, I was at a loss for how adult women socialised. I hovered around the fringes of social groups, watching as other mums made dates for coffee or shopping. They seemed so at ease, as if they'd all gotten the Mum Handbook, whilst my copy had been lost in the mail.

I probably should have been envious but I was too busy being intimidated.

*

Asperger syndrome provided an explanation but not a solution when it came to socialising. I've had friends over the years, but not, it seems, in the way that other women do. Fortunately, I've made one friend who has been a constant in my adult life: my husband Sang.

Again and again as I was researching Asperger syndrome in adults, I came across bleak portraits of adult relationships. Broken marriages. Impossible-to-live-with autistic spouses.

Many of the challenges described in the literature were familiar. Our marriage certainly hasn't been easy. But learning that I'm autistic has given us a new framework for understanding our relationship. Everything from why I find social outings exhausting to why I need to eat the same thing for breakfast every day suddenly had an explanation.

That understanding alone is a tremendous gift. People often question why someone my age would bother getting diagnosed, especially someone who has a job, a family, and a mostly-settled path in life.

The explanation that comes with a diagnosis makes all the difference. For years, I knew something was wrong with me but I had no idea what. Most of the possibilities that I came up with made me feel bad about myself. Cold. Unfeeling. Immature. Selfish. Short-tempered. Defective.

My diagnosis swept all of those aside. Not only did I get an explanation for how I experience life, I got a user's guide to my brain. It wasn't an endpoint in my journey, but a starting place.

*

There was joy in that realisation and also sadness. My diagnosis came too late to help me in my role as a mother when my daughter was young; a role that I often struggled with. Many aspects of being autistic can make the child-rearing years of motherhood challenging.

Babies have around-the-clock needs. They're stressful, messy, unpredictable and demanding. Basically they are everything that an autistic person finds hard to cope with. Gone was my precious alone time. Gone were my carefully crafted routines. Even my body was no longer my own, transformed first by pregnancy then by postpartum hormones and breastfeeding.

I was completely unprepared for how hard motherhood would be. Unaware that I was autistic, I often felt like a bad mum. What kind of mother breaks down sobbing uncontrollably and bangs her head against the dining room wall? Certainly none that I was aware of at the time.

Perhaps knowing why I was having so many meltdowns - or even having a proper word for those scary sobbing, head banging episodes - would have made the early days of motherhood easier. Perhaps knowing that I have a social communication impairment would have pushed me to understand why it's important for a mother to frequently say "I love you" to her child.

When I told my daughter about my early suspicions that I might be an aspie, initially she found it hard to believe. As we talked more, she slowly came around, at first agreeing with the traits I put forward, and then beginning to offer up other aspects of me that fit the female ASD profile I'd shared with her.

Since then, we've talked about what my ASD means; how it's impacted her as my daughter, and how it influences our interactions. We've also agreed that it isn't all bad. Far from it.

I wasn't a traditional mum, but I think I managed to not mess up the important stuff. We had rules and routines, though sometimes too many. We played and read together and watched *The Sound of Music* every time it ran on TV. We raised a dog and loved her and cried together when she died. I taught her to cook and to drive and told her it was okay to do her algebra homework in a way that made sense to her, no matter what her teacher said.

But when it came to girl stuff, I was mostly clueless. It was easy at first: dresses and pigtails, dolls and tea parties. Toy stores make it obvious which toys are the "girl" toys. As she got older, I tried to interest her in the things I'd enjoyed as a kid but she had little interest in Lego and was easily bored by the detailed instructions I so loved following. She liked baking and playing video games. She liked to paint and do craft projects, creating art from anything she could get her hands on.

Words and watercolours and scraps of yarn kept her busy for hours while I looked on in puzzlement. I don't have an artistic bone in my body and a blank canvas sends a shiver of fear down my spine. It was fascinating to watch as my daughter grew into a young woman who was both very much like me and a completely independent person.

She picked out her own clothes, chose her own hairstyles, took up the guitar and developed a love of poetry. I don't know where she learned about make-up and nail polish and which shoes go with what skirt or how to match jewellery to an outfit. It wasn't from me. In fact, I'm the one who asks her for fashion advice. She's remarkably good at it and remarkably girly, and that makes me smile.

Still, I look at her and see so much of myself. She has my passion for what she believes in. She has my directness and honesty, my attachment to the truth. She definitely has my sense of humour - one that few others get. She has my practicality and frugalness, my drive for perfection and my tenacity. She has my independent spirit, secure in who she is in ways that I wasn't at her age.

Never once has she hinted that I wasn't a good mother. She sees the best in me and always has.

I'm not sure who or what is responsible for that, but I'd like to think her dad and I are, at least partially. I'd like to think that even without the benefit of a diagnosis, I managed to do that most important of things - raising a child - well enough.

*

Increasingly I'm making my peace with not seeing myself in traditional role models. I've always known that I wasn't a typical female. My presentation is atypical - from the way I dress to my crew cut - but so are my interests.

Again and again I've found myself in male-dominated environments: the Economics department where I did my undergraduate degree, the martial arts schools where I earned a black belt and later taught, and the shooting range where I learned the finer points of target shooting.

Autism is often framed as a male condition. The original diagnostic criteria were primarily based on studies of boys. The diagnostic rate is many times higher for males than for females. There is even a theory suggesting that autistic women are "more male" based on thinking styles. The psychologist who diagnosed me, noting my presentation and interests, suggested I look into the extreme male brain theory to see if it was a good fit.

Does ASD predispose women toward typically masculine traits? Would I find economics, sparring or target shooting as interesting if I wasn't autistic? What about shopping or fashion? Does being autistic prevent me from liking typically feminine interests?

Those questions are impossible to answer.

However, I can look around at the other autistic women I know for clues. Some of them are interested in traditionally male pursuits like martial arts and fencing and gaming. Some are interested in more traditionally female pastimes like baking and knitting. Some are scientists and mathematicians: historically male-dominated roles. Others are teachers or social workers: traditionally nurturing professions. Few have a love of fashion or shopping, but some enjoy it quite a lot.

Ultimately, we are individuals, influenced by being autistic and influenced by being female, but in the end still individuals.

*

Perhaps rather than extreme male brains, autistic women have extreme individual brains. As a group we seem to be less influenced than typical women by the roles society expects us to play.

As a child, I had little concept of gender roles. I liked what I liked, regardless of how socially appropriate my interests were. I played with Barbies and Legos, Lincoln Logs and Tinker Toys, Little People, Weebles, Spirograph, Fashion Plates, Hot Wheels, and board games. My Barbies rode around in their plastic mobile home, past my model train set and my slot car race track. No one told me there were boys' toys and girls' toys.

In fifth grade (when I was about 10), a friend asked what I wanted for my birthday. When I said Lego, she said I needed to grow up because soon I would be "changing" and wouldn't like "things like that" anymore. I felt like she knew something I didn't. That scared me but I was undeterred.

I liked Lego. I also liked *M*A*S*H* and collecting coins and shooting hoops. I liked sewing and making pottery. I had a punching bag hanging from the ceiling in the basement and a well-worn baseball mitt. I liked romance novels and horror novels, Nancy Drew and logic puzzles. I hung photos of rock stars in my high school locker then went home and pretended I was an outlaw as I shot cans off a stump in the backyard with my BB gun.

My interests were both typical and atypical for a girl my age. Sometimes this bothered me, like when my friend ominously (and incorrectly) predicted I'd lose interest in Lego. Most of the time, though, I did what I liked regardless of what others thought. At some point, I guess I just resigned myself to being seen as the geeky girl.

Like many autistic kids, I also missed a lot of the social byplay that happened among my peers. If I was supposed to be modelling myself primarily on my female friends, I never got that message.

I modelled myself on people that I liked and admired. Sometimes those people were female and sometimes they were male.

I picked up interests based on how interesting they were, regardless of whether they were socially acceptable for girls or even for kids. At nine, I was the only child in a sewing class for adults. Apparently there were no sewing classes for children so my parents found an adult class that would have me. Off I went each week, with my sewing kit and a wooden block that raised my sewing machine pedal a foot off the ground so my foot could reach it. The middle-aged women in the class thought I was an adorable curiosity.

It never occurred to me that this was unusual. My extreme individual brain likes what it likes. It always has.

*

While many of the intersections of autistic and female in my life have been social, there are undeniable physical intersections too.

The arrival of adolescence brought with it hints of what it would mean to be an autistic adult. My first real meltdowns. My first experience with depression. My first confusing encounters with physical intimacy.

With nothing to compare those experiences to, I assumed they were a normal part of teenage life. Everyone said that being a teenager was hard, I couldn't dispute that and it didn't seem necessary to look beyond the explanation of "this is hard for everyone."

That would become a theme. Pregnancy. Breastfeeding. Postpartum depression. My body's reaction to birth control pills. Countless books and magazine articles assured me that these things were no walk in the park. Not knowing that I was autistic, I had no idea that I might be having a rougher time of it than the average woman.

It wasn't until I hit menopause - and the hormonal fireworks that come with it - that I finally realised something was different. Not just with how I was responding to the hormonal changes of perimenopause, but with how I was coping with life in general.

At first, I had no idea that perimenopause had begun. It crept up slowly and because I was barely out of my thirties, the word menopause wasn't part of my vocabulary. What I noticed, instead, was that I was having a lot of difficulty coping with the daily demands of life. It was harder to concentrate on work. I wasn't sleeping well and felt tired all of the time. I was moody and quick to cry over the silliest things. But the most surprising development was a new resistance to socialising. Being around people I don't know well had always been uncomfortable, but suddenly it felt exhausting.

Ultimately, thanks to the hormonal changes of perimenopause, my autistic traits became too obvious to ignore. This led, in a roundabout way, to my realisation that I'm on the spectrum. And that feels like a fitting sequence of events, because the cognitive challenges of menopause are turning out to be much greater than the physical symptoms. Yes, the irregular periods, night sweats and sleep disturbances are hard. But it's what's happening in my brain - the way "the change" is changing my cognitive function - that's taken centre stage for me.

Forgetfulness, concentration problems, anxiety, fatigue and mood swings are often listed among the "other symptoms" of perimenopause. Thanks to my autistic brain, I already experience those things to a greater degree than the average woman. Menopause has ramped up the intensity, but I've had years to develop coping strategies.

The symptom I've struggled the most with is one that you won't find on any typical list of symptoms. Three years into perimenopause, my language processing has developed some glitches. When I write, I leave out words and make odd substitutions. Speaking is an adventure in trying to remember which noun I'm looking for.

At first, I thought maybe my brain was broken in some new and scary way. When I blogged about my worsening language glitches, I was stunned to hear from dozens of autistic women in their forties and fifties who had similar experiences. Other discussions on menopause revealed more common ground. I wasn't the only one who was suddenly tired of the effort it takes to pass for "normal". I wasn't the only one having more meltdowns or struggling to cope with day-to-day responsibilities. There were a lot of "me too" replies, too many for them to be a coincidence.

The autistic female body is fundamentally different, it seems. We start out with an atypical baseline. Add in hormonal fluctuations and we get *Menopause: The Deluxe Bonus Edition*. Thankfully, I finally have what I lacked during those other hard stages of my life: community. I have other women - women like me - whose experiences I can look to for comfort and wisdom.

*

Throughout my life, being autistic has shaped my experience of being female. But how has being a woman shaped my experience of being autistic?

Because I'm new to being autistic - that is, to knowing I'm autistic - this is a harder question to answer. My autistic traits are an indelible part of me and always have been. Whether I was aware of them as autistic or not, they influenced me at every stage of my life. Now that I recognise their autistic nature, I can look back and see how they have made me who I am.

Perhaps the greatest impact of gender has been that it helped to cloak my autism. I grew up in a time before Asperger syndrome existed. Children of my generation were much less likely to be diagnosed with autism if they could speak and were in a mainstream classroom.

My teachers realised early on that I was different from the other kids. They labelled me gifted and designed a special curriculum to keep me busy. They enrolled me in the town's gifted classes. They tasked me with helping out the reading specialist and the librarian. They even tried to skip me over a grade, a move that my parents wisely blocked, reasoning that my already painfully shy nature would put me at too big of a disadvantage with kids two years older than me.

Even as an adult, autism was a hard explanation to consider. I skirted it for years, buying into the Rain Man stereotype, not seeing myself in the descriptions of boys who loved aeroplane engines and men who had no social lives. It wasn't until I discovered Tony Attwood's writing that I realised there is more than one way to be autistic.

Girls can be autistic too. In fact, there was a detail in Dr Attwood's book that made me gasp out loud. In explaining how autistic girls often have interests that appear to be the same as typical girls, he described how one of his patients liked to play with Barbies, but instead of making up pretend scenarios for them, she enjoyed lining up the dolls and their clothes.

I felt like I'd been struck by lightning. I had a huge collection of mostly hand-me-down Barbies and their clothing, and what I most loved doing was laying all of the items out on my bedroom floor and sorting them by type. I had far less interest in dressing the Barbies or sending them on dates than in ensuring that each of them had exactly the same number of dresses and pants and shirts and shoes. I could spend hours sorting and distributing their clothes. Once that was done, I'd play with them for five minutes and pack everything away until next time.

If an adult walked by and glanced in my room, they would have seen a little girl playing with her dolls. Only if they'd watched carefully would they have noticed that I did the exact same thing every time. Classic autistic behaviour camouflaged in a girly disguise. If I'd been a boy with a love of sorting batteries or radio parts, my autistic traits may have been more noticeable.

As girls, we learn to hide in plain sight. We hover at the fringes of social groups, giving the impression that we have friends. We sit quietly through years of school, creating the illusion of shyness.

We let older girls take us under their wings, mothering and mentoring us in the social skills that they sense we're lacking. We learn that there are rules and we set out to master them as best we can. We learn that we have roles to play and we struggle to fill them, often at the cost of our self-esteem.

*

Coming to understand that autistic girls and women have somewhat different traits than autistic boys and men made it clear, finally, that there was a place on the spectrum for me. Not only that, there were other women like me, other women who shared similar traits and experiences.

I'd spent decades feeling like I was an anomaly and suddenly here was an entire community of people who understood.

As I've read the experiences of other autistic women, I've come to realise why autism is described as a spectrum condition. As autistic people, we share much in common but we are also different in many ways. No one is autistic in exactly the same way that I am. This has given me permission to be me - to see myself on the broad spectrums of womanhood and humanity - and to embrace myself as I am.

I'd like to say this is a done deal - I've accepted myself and now I can move on, brandishing my shiny new self-image. Perhaps that will be the case one day, but for now, I am a work in progress. Each time I think "Yes, this is it, I've got it now" I soon find myself unpeeling a new layer, discovering some aspect of myself that I'd tucked safely away.

In the past year, I have rediscovered the joy of stimming. I have unearthed a playfulness within me that I thought was lost. I have begun to learn how to share my feelings and speak up for myself and identify my wants and needs. I've opened up doors inside me that I was once frightened of even approaching.

There is a joy and a terror in this kind of self-discovery that is akin to the best roller coaster ride ever. Again and again I find myself nervously climbing that first hill, anxiously anticipating the first drop and then, finally, with a shout of joy, giving myself over to the thrill of the ride.

Chapter 3
Alison Wattis

Alison is 19 years old. She was diagnosed with Asperger syndrome when she was 18. She enjoys a wide range of activities, from drawing and painting, to learning about Greek mythology, to cake decorating and cross stitch. She is pictured here as a child with her pet dog (and best friend) Bella.

Where shall I begin? My name is Alison and I was diagnosed two years ago now. A strange girl, who dances to Adam and the Ants, dresses in bright clothing and was terrified of vacuum cleaners (due to my high sensory sensitivities). I was a child who constantly needed to retreat into their own world. In fact, I still do it now. I will read books, play video games, anything so long as I am not left alone with my mind. As a child I was sick. A lot. To begin with I had meningitis (when doctors gave me a lumbar puncture to test me they took out too much fluid – my GP told my mum that I was lucky I didn't get brain damage), then I had bronchitis, many chest infections and also cysts which required lancing. Thus I saw the interior of my local hospital quite regularly and went through periods of time when I wasn't at school and when I was, my mum had to come to give me medication. Anyway, my point is I didn't get much chance to socialise with other children, though when I did I got on with them pretty well. I tended to play more with the boys than the girls. This was thanks to my two cousins, who were both boys, that I played with every Saturday (even a sickly girl might prefer to play fight rather than talk about dresses and dolls). I did have another cousin, who was a girl; however she was older than me and liked to be with the adults so I didn't see her much. Even now I find myself having more in common with boys than girls.

I was considered odd, as I tended to prefer my own company. I read books even before school and didn't talk much either. I remember when I first realised that I was "different". I was about seven at the time; I was in class at school and our teacher had given us an activity. We all had to sit in a circle on the floor. The teacher sat with us and had a pile of pencils in front of her. She told us to pass one pencil at a time to the person next to us in a conveyer belt action until she had all the pencils again. Everyone did as they were told but I couldn't keep up. They were all telling me to hurry up but I just couldn't do it fast enough. I broke down and cried. I wasn't embarrassed as I don't have the ability to feel that way; however I was angry - angry that I had made myself look so silly.

I find myself frequently daydreaming. I can remember dreaming about being a pirate or being an adventurer, but my most frequent dream was being in an orchestra, usually playing the piano or the harp. It was the dream I yearned for the most. I would daydream about it and then I would dream about it at night. I kept pestering my parents for lessons, but we aren't a rich family and we were never able to afford them. I was getting desperate until one day an opportunity came up - I could take violin lessons provided by my school. This was my chance to prove how much I wanted this dream, to show that I could be good at it. I thought to myself "maybe I could be one of those musicians who create such beautiful sounds". I put my hand up for the teacher to see, straining so hard I thought my arm was going to pop out of its socket. We were told to wait for a day until the school had made their decision. I was so restless that I couldn't think straight. I was sure I would have a chance, my obsession with music was obvious - it was one of the few things I could talk about in plenty. The day came and I was nervous, but when the chosen names were announced, mine was not one of them. I pushed past the heartache and painful disappointment, but with it began the anger which I have had to fight so hard against since then. A few years later, at the same school, I was given another chance. Group keyboard lessons were being offered so I put my name down and this time I was allowed. For those lessons, I would have to stay behind and bring my own keyboard. I was happy to do so, as it meant a chance to finally prove that I could do this. It might not have been the most glamorous start, but it was a start nonetheless. I even gave up dancing lessons, something which I was happy doing and was already getting good at, to pursue the keyboard lessons. I started the lessons and was enjoying every moment of it. Sadly after two lessons they were stopped as demand for them was too low. I still pestered my parents for lessons and spent a few nights (perhaps more than a few) crying about it but I refused to give up on that hope. I have since resolved to never attempt music lessons from a school again.

When I was at primary school I was content, I knew the pupils and they knew me and even though I was treated unfairly by my teachers (a long and boring story), I wasn't treated differently by the other children because I had grown up with them so they just saw me as being myself. They understood that but the adults around me were a different story. I was constantly being picked on for my behaviour by my teachers. They would moan to my parents at parent's evening: "your daughter is too quiet" and "she never puts her hand up in class when she needs help". My parents would constantly tell them "that is how she is" but it didn't work and this would be a recurring "problem" that I was singled out for throughout my school life. I later explained to my parents that it is just how I have to learn, I need to learn by myself because if someone does it for me, even if they show me what to do, I can't remember it.

Then came secondary school and my family would say "you will be fine once you've settled in". They reassured me that others had found it difficult at first but "after a month they were fine". How wrong they were, the problem being that I had to go to a different school to everyone else from my primary school. Picture this: a young, socially awkward, nervous girl who acts and dresses different to everyone around her. It went about as well as can be expected on my first day; some people wouldn't talk to me but others teased and bullied me. I had this from my teachers before, but never from other pupils. I was terrified. I was all alone in a place I had never been before and without anyone to help. I had never felt so isolated and the loneliness has stuck with me ever since. The bullying continued; every day I would be emotionally and mentally tormented. The boys never bothered with me - I was just a quiet girl so they were never that interested - but the girls were another matter. I was constantly being picked up on for how I looked. I have never had an interest in wearing make-up - I don't like it personally so I never put it on. I never make a special effort on my hair, I look after it but I don't style it, just a quick wash, brush and air dry and it is fine. Yet I was always treated like I was dirty all the time for it, they would call me "gross" or similar things. I would be made fun of because I have full lips or because my eyes were too big – anything that could be brought attention to. Then they would whisper behind my back in class (making sure to say only my name loud enough to hear) and then when I turned around they would giggle at me, which made me paranoid. The only way I could see this ending was by making my own friends. This worked for a while but before long they started stealing from me and one even wrote hurtful gossip on a bathroom wall for everyone to see. I tried getting in with certain groups such as the girls who wore eyeliner and listened to rubbish rock bands (I grew up with rock classics). Again, it worked for a while but they didn't respect me and they tried to get me into shoplifting, so I broke away from them. So there I was again, alone and in torment, slowly going insane - whenever I was around people I could hear whispering when there wasn't any. I couldn't sleep and when I did I had nightmares (I would have nightmares every night as a child).

Now, for the next part, I need to tell you a story.

When I was little I went swimming with two of my cousins. It is important for you to know I couldn't swim until I was about eleven and at this point in time I was about five. So I was in the pool along with the boy cousin. I was in shallow end and the girl was walking around the edge. I don't remember how it happened or how it ended but at some point I ended up underneath the water unable to swim to the surface so I just sank down. I remember everything being blue, I don't remember people swimming above me. I was completely alone and unable to breathe. I should have been scared, what with me being a nervous wreck and all, but I just felt calm and so at peace. I often think about that time in my darkest moments.

So now I have finished my story I can continue. I was in a predicament at school because I had no-one to help me navigate around (it was a large school and I would often turn up to class late by accident) and no-one to keep me company (even if it was bad company). The bullying was getting worse and so too was my anxiety; it goes straight to my stomach and makes me nauseous. I was often sent home from school because I was too sick to carry on with the day. My parents found out about the bullying and went to the school. Teachers showed me a photo and asked me to point out the bullies. I refused because I knew exactly what they were planning to do. They thought they could just have a word with the bullies, have them suspended for a while and then everything would be fine. If there are any teachers reading this, listen to me now: getting a child to point out bullies and talking to them is not going to help. I have seen it first hand; you are doing far more harm than good. The bullying gets worse, it gets more frequent and more brutal. All you are doing is giving the bullies more to work with and giving them more reason to continue. Sorry, just needed to get that out.

So everything was getting worse. I couldn't find any solace at home either because now my parents were starting to argue with me. They would always ask "Why can't you tell me what is going on?", not understanding that I couldn't. I started to feel defective, like I was broken or a piece of me was missing. Then I started thinking back to that time where I was so calm. I was having a bath at the time and I thought "why don't I do it again?", but this time stay there and then I can be calm again. Except this time it would be forever, rather than a brief moment. I went to put my head underneath the water but when it got to my nose, I realized what I was doing. I pulled myself up and just sat there thinking about what I had considered doing. I thought that I could keep myself in check and I wasn't going to tell my parents. I didn't want them to be worried. However, as hard as I tried I couldn't stop myself from having those thoughts. I would look at the contents in the medicine cupboard and the knives in the kitchen drawer, they started to look a lot more comforting than they did before and it scared me. After a particularly awful day at school I decided, whilst my parents were out shopping, that I was going to raid the medicine cupboard and leave a note for them. I had already decided what I was going to say. Luckily, I didn't go through with it, as when I got home my mum was in the kitchen. Instead I told her what had happened and revealed how I had been feeling. Then, I am not kidding, she pulled me out of school that very day. I couldn't believe it; I have never felt such a surge of relief. I am not going to lie, I still had those thoughts, but now there was a small glimmer of hope of a better life. It was just enough to keep me fighting. If you are having feelings like I did, I am not going to patronise you and promise you that everything will definitely get better. However, you need to find something worth fighting for. It is there, you might have lost sight of it or you didn't notice it before, but there is always something worth fighting for. I'll be honest, it is a long, hard crawl back, but you can get there. I am the proof you need, I couldn't write this here and now if I hadn't pulled myself out of those murky waters.

I got moved out of that school and into another - a school for children with behavioural problems. I got into that school via my GP. My parents said that I couldn't cope at my current school so my GP contacted the new school and I got in. It was quieter, the classes were smaller, I made and lost more "friends". However, I needed even quieter classes because even though the classes were only of about ten people, they were still very noisy. So my parents and I needed to fight again to get me into home teaching. I still went into school every day but the days were shorter and I was in classes of about four. I was finally content once more.

Then when I was watching the television one night with my parents, a popular medical programme on Channel Four came on. It was about people who had a condition called Asperger syndrome. I knew nothing about it, I hadn't even heard of it before. The common symptoms seemed familiar, they were the same things that I thought were my defects. I told my parents and they just laughed it off. However things were adding up and I knew. I wanted to be sure so I filled in an online quiz they have and I got a severe rating. So I told my parents who told a psychologist that I was going to see in a few weeks and he said that I did show symptoms. He then talked to his superior and she said that I was "too complacent" and that I would "answer questions" they gave me so I didn't have Asperger syndrome. I have since come to understand that this is a load of rubbish. However, my parents believed her so I had to convince them all over again. I managed to do that by printing off the quiz I did again (and got same results). We then had to convince my GP but he laughed it off, so we changed GP. My new GP put me through to a different psychologist who agreed that I showed symptoms. She asked if I wanted a diagnosis. I told her I did and I got it. Other than a few recommended books I got no help. So I did a little surfing on the internet and came across an organisation called Autism West Midlands (the people putting this book together for you). They offered help for me to be able to understand why I act differently to others. It is worth checking if you have similar support on offer near you, however if you don't there are lots of stories from others like me online which can also help. Recently I have applied to a specialist college to study art. I have met the teachers who seem to like me and think I would be happy there (I do too). I am hoping to get funding so that I can attend this college. I have also started piano lessons! I had my first exam recently and passed with a distinction (the highest level you can get!). So even though it took time and effort and it seemed like it was all for nothing, in the end I am still following my dream and so can you. Whether you are autistic or not, I hope this chapter has helped you in some way because we are two sides of the same coin.

Chapter 4
Esther Whitney

My name is Esther Whitney. I am 26 years old and I have Asperger syndrome which is an Autistic Spectrum Disorder. I have just completed a degree in Visual Arts at Birmingham City University. Most of my artwork communicates my daily struggles with living with Asperger's and all the anxiety which goes alongside the condition. I struggle to communicate on a social level with people so I use my skills in art to have my say and communicate the way I see the world.

There is a triad of impairments in autism; my idea is to create a piece of artwork for each element of the triad. I want to be able to help others understand the difficulties people who are on the autistic spectrum face on a day-to-day basis by using my skills in art.

Since getting a diagnosis of Asperger syndrome I have been on a mission to work through all of the emotions that come with a diagnosis; suddenly everything starts to make sense. Having a diagnosis answered lots of questions, but it also raised a lot of questions. I want to express how I feel about having a developmental disorder by creating artwork that shows the difficulties I have; and how I can overcome those difficulties through the power of art.

Raining Cats and Dogs
Literal Thinking

Objective: I want to create a piece of art which shows that people on the autistic spectrum think in pictures and become confused with metaphors because they take what people say literally. I have chosen to look at the metaphor 'raining cats and dogs'. When I first heard this, I actually thought it was raining cats and dogs! It is like my brain just won't decode it as quickly as other people do.

"A person with Asperger syndrome may not have the flexibility of thought to understand an alternative meaning and relies on logic rather than symbolism, and the assumption that the other person is saying exactly what he or she means."

- Dr Tony Attwood

In this project my inspiration is codes, to me metaphors are like codes - they are very confusing. As someone who takes what people say very literally I get very confused when people use metaphors.

My intention is to make the audience initially confused. They are then free to decode the metaphors by interacting, whether that is walking around or touching the cubes. The audience then has a chance to work it out, just like when a person with autism hears a metaphor and gets confused. I am confusing people who normally confuse me. I want people to think. I want the viewer to have a 'eureka' moment when they realise what autism is about. This idea represents the notion that people with autism think differently to people who do not have autism. I have used black and white cubes and symbols to represent the theory that people who are on the autistic spectrum have 'black and white thinking'.

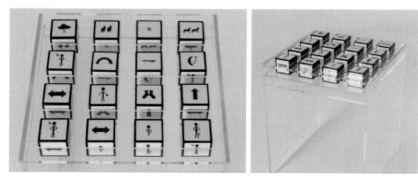

Acrylic, timber, black gloss paint and vinyl stickers
Sculpture by Esther Whitney
Photographer by Graham Purcell

The Mirror Neuron Theory
Asperger Syndrome and Social Understanding

Objective: For the flexibility of thought impairment I am looking at the mirror neuron theory. We all have mirror neurons in the frontal lobe part of our brains. Mirror neurons are in charge of mirroring others' expressions, feelings and emotions. Mirror neurons give us the ability to understand other people's actions. They act as a guide to understanding the behaviour of others by referring back to our own personal beliefs and experiences to form a guess as to what is going on in another person's mind. The theory is that people on the autistic spectrum have mirror neurons which are not as high functioning as those in non-autistics. Someone with autism may be able to imitate a facial expression, but with no emotional connection to it. This makes it difficult for them to relate to others.

Acrylic, gum tape and LED lights
Sculpture by Esther Whitney
Photographs by Graham Bradbury

There are three mirror neurons. Two of the mirror neurons fire blue electrical signals but the mirror neuron in the middle is not firing, this shows that the mirror neurons in people who are on the autistic spectrum are not working properly. People with autism might not have a natural understanding of mirroring, but we can learn how to react to others. I have encased the mirror neurons inside an egg. Most people associate eggs with new life and I want this idea to be a new way of thinking about autism; that a lot of positives can come out of it!

A Thimble Full
Asperger Syndrome and Social Difficulties

The idea for A Thimble Full developed after reading the following quotation from Dr Tony Attwood.

'Many people on the autistic spectrum may need a "thimble" of socialising instead of the big oversized sixty-four ounce gulper that many "normal" people seek out.'

Having always wanted to produce a piece of art in relation to the difficulties Asperger's creates when socialising, I decided to produce a visual and educational piece expressing my experience of social interaction when combined with Asperger's syndrome.

Attwood's idea about socialising made me think about how we understand social interaction. After researching various dictionary definitions of what it means 'to socialise', I decided that my view of social interaction was in fact very simple; you say something and the other person says something in response. Noticing that there was a pattern involved, I wondered whether it could be simplified into some sort of social formula.

On contacting Professor David Needham at Birmingham University, he provided me with a model formula demonstrating social interaction in people with Asperger's and people without Asperger's. The formula showed the difficulties people with Asperger's have when faced with social situations. Socialising can present a major difficulty for people with Asperger's who often find it hard to read people. It is not by any means that they do not wish to socialise, however many find that it can be easier not to, finding people unpredictable and confusing.

A Thimble Full is made up of three specially cast silver thimbles, each engraved with the social formula for people with Asperger's. Each has been filled with a resin and contains precious gems, symbolising the few, close friendships I have had in my life so far. Like the stones each friendship is precious, because for each friend I have made, I have had to overcome the barriers Asperger's has put in the way.

The gems were chosen in accordance with their symbolism in relation to communication and relationships: Sapphire (believed to help with communication), Topaz (ability to grasp high level concepts, confidence and personal power), Diamond (amplifies thoughts of the user), Aquamarine (gives courage and enhances communications skills), and Lapis Lazuli (believed to be the gem of love, friendship and truth as encourages harmony in relationships).

The first thimble stands tall, full of the resin and gems. The second thimble is falling; illustrating the times I have said or done something inappropriate because of the difficulty I have with socialising. The third thimble has fallen, the precious gems spilling out. Each thimble stands in an acrylic box, demonstrating how I have captured each precious friendship and have frozen them in a piece of artwork.

In July 2011 A Thimble Full won the national Create! Art for Autism competition and as a result was displayed in the Houses of Parliament in March 2012.

Sliver, resin, acrylic and gems
Sculpture by Esther Whitney
Photographs by Graham Bradbury

Social Formula

This is a painting of the mathematical formula I used on the thimbles; this formula relates to a graph which shows the difficulties people on the autistic spectrum have with making friends over a period of time.

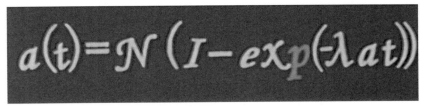

$$a(t) = \mathcal{N}\left(I - exp(-\lambda a t)\right)$$

Acrylic on canvas

Everything has a place
Routines

People with Asperger's may have different topics and routines that they must follow through. It is not that we are being difficult; it is that we are behaving in a way that is logical in our minds.

I hate mess! Everything in my flat has its very own home. I am always cleaning and tidying, making sure that everything is in the right place. I get very angry if people do not put things back in the right places or leave things in a mess. I need to feel that I am in control, when my flat is organised, clean and tidy, I am happy and I can go about my daily routines without much disruption. It does become a bit obsessive from time to time. I could never be messy or disorganised because my brain just would never allow it.

The only way that I could tolerate mess is in a controlled environment and by the mess having its own place. I want to present my obsession visually; to do this I have used three acrylic cubes because the cubes have a lid and they are a controlled environment. Each time I vacuumed I collected the dust and stored it inside the three acrylic cubes. I have displayed the three acrylic cubes on a white floating shelf as if they were ornaments in a home. The distance between each box has been measured out accurately which suggests my obsessive nature.

Floating shelf with three acrylic boxes filled with dust

Chapter 5
Noushka Woszczylo

Noushka was diagnosed with high functioning autism when she was 6. Despite huge struggles during her childhood, she did not let her learning difference hinder her academic, physical or social abilities.

Freelancing as a children's book illustrator, Noushka likes to collect hats and picture books. She has also written and illustrated the picture book "Escape", and an a-z introduction to autism.

Noushka is always on the lookout for ways to help others through the medium of drawing. Whether to raise money for charity, or inform and advise people who are at a loss with a health or social problem.

Could you start by telling me about your experiences at school and your diagnosis?

I was put in a mainstream nursery that couldn't cope with learning disabilities at all. This environment exposed my autism at the lowest end of the spectrum because the teachers frightened me. This continued into primary school. My mum underwent copious amounts of scrutiny and adversity from medics until we met a paediatrician and a children's psychologist. My paediatrician diagnosed me with high-functioning autism and I received a statement of special educational needs when I was aged 6. I was then transferred to a special school. Academically, I was about 2 years ahead because things were taken at a manageable pace for all the pupils. I was put up two years for some classes but my priority was to learn social skills. Sadly, as soon as I completed a year and befriended classmates, I was deemed capable of attending mainstream school. I was bullied to the point of near suicide in primary and secondary school and didn't make many close friends in college. It had been easier for me to make friends in the special school I went to because there were others on the spectrum. We all got along because difference was welcomed, even amongst the pupils.

In mainstream school, I found I was a magnet for bullies because I didn't quite fit in and only had a very basic sense of humour. That was a vicious cycle that I wish I could have got out of but I didn't know what to do nor was I assertive enough to say anything to put people off. I had a fresh start at each school but it always ended the same until college. College was a relief because I didn't experience bullying there. Everyone has a reason to be there. University is even better because it's international. There are a lot of different people and disabilities are welcomed for the diversity they bring. I think people almost admire you if there is something different about you because it means that you have overcome things to get to university.

Did your teachers know about your problems at school?

Yes they knew I had a statement. I went to the ECM manager (Every Child Matters) and the SENCO (Special Educational Needs Co-ordinator) at my school about the bullying but they kept saying "just ignore and avoid them" and didn't give me any practical help. Of course, even following this advice didn't help. It just encouraged people to bully me more because I didn't put up a fight. So I absorbed insults and by the time I got to college I burnt out in second year from putting myself under so much pressure and from the eating disorder I was struggling with. I developed this to cope with a life I just couldn't fit in with.

The grades I achieved indicated a healthy and smart pupil with a promising future. No member of staff ever looked past the numbers to see how badly I coped with the school environment. This tunnel vision that schools live by makes staff blind to hidden conditions like autism. It would come home with me and I would work through the night and get myself in a real state. Even with small pop quizzes I would have a meltdown for the whole week beforehand. When I got back to school the next week I would still get 100% even though I had a lot of difficulties with exam pressure at school. Because I take everything literally and personally, I over-worked throughout my education. I had to take a year out of university because I was completely overwhelmed by the pressure to get good results. When teachers and tutors were talking to people who weren't doing well (usually the underachievers who were bullying me), they really emphasised the importance of getting good exam results. In response, I would take the whole world on my shoulders and think I had to do 1000%.

I chose a vocational course at college. My exam mentality did not match up well with the practical aspect of the course. I had been advised by my college not to choose an academic course if I planned to go to university afterwards. However, I was effectively putting in twice the amount of academic work for half the grades that the tutors were really interested in. I was working with vocational deadlines so didn't have the exam challenge but the deadlines and the workload within each project were just as challenging. Proportionally I put myself under double the pressure - one of my many self-destructive ways of coping. It got me through my exams but then I didn't fare so well on the vocational course so I had to take a short break and then cram my degree show (where I produced the work I would go on to showcase) into the last week of term.

Can you tell me how making friends impacted your perception of loneliness?

As a young child, loneliness wasn't a concept that occurred to me. I never felt it and no one thought to mention it to me because it's not something you talk about to a four-year-old. I was fine until I made my first group of friends. I actually had two or three friends by the end of my time at my special school - it was a really safe school - but when I integrated back into mainstream school I had an awareness of isolation for the first time. It was an alien feeling and something that was quite hard to come to terms with.

When I was young, my whole world was just Lego. I was happy playing with it all day every day for quite a few years. When I got to school I was quite happy to not have friends because making friends is difficult and I'd gone without friends for long enough. But my school told me to stretch myself and try to interact with people. Now that I've made friends it's really hard to go back on it because the feelings of isolation are so massive. It's all or nothing. It's very black and white in an autistic world. Looking back, I think it was good to make friends because I wouldn't have the interaction skills I need to speak over the phone, for example. With a disembodied voice, I tend to panic if I'm given a question that I didn't expect, but I think it would be a lot worse if I hadn't learnt how to make friends.

What are your interests?

I tend to be interested in really weird stuff like archery and chess. Not many people really get involved with that. I have to be careful in what I tell about myself depending on the social circle I am with at the time. I like to work all the time so I bring my laptop everywhere; it makes it harder to interact with people but easier for me overall because interaction leaves me quite lethargic. In the last few months I've come across a bit of a problem where I have to go out and speak to someone at least once a day otherwise I feel really isolated. I can get into a zone where I'm working or reading or doing something all day. But then I don't want to do anything else and I get locked into doing that one activity for weeks at a time. If I don't have that, there's nothing to occupy me which makes me quite aware that I'm not with any friends. I've got a fixation on clay at the moment; I make a lot of clay jewellery. It's encouraging because it's a task where I can interact with people by showing, selling and giving things away at the end. I love to be productive when I'm doing solitary tasks. The finished products give me an incentive to start interacting again which is a nice balance between having time to myself and time with friends. It's a challenge to find stuff to keep me from feeling isolated. Private things like eating and shopping I'm OK with but if I have a whole 3 days completely on my own I do struggle to keep myself company.

Could you tell me about your friendships and relationships?

Women are encouraged to hang out with groups of their own gender but I just find it simpler to hang out with guys. Being the age I am, it's something that my mum doesn't approve of, naturally, but normal girls are quite complicated. There's a whole subliminal language that no one seems to know about; it's not even written down. The majority of my friends are guys. I can find it quite difficult comprehending people's reactions, hand gestures and tone of voice. Girls are even harder to understand: they tend to use more sarcasm and are very indirect. Some of my friends are also diagnosed with Asperger's. I do have a mix of sort of "normal" friends too but it's harder to keep up with what they do because there's so much more interaction. When people with autism get in a big group, everybody's got their task. We're all together keeping each other company but we're all in our own little worlds as well. That's quite a bit simpler.

I was engaged to someone for a few months that I met at university. He wasn't diagnosed but showed all of the autistic traits. That didn't really work out so I took a break. I called it off because I was overworking and making myself ill at uni and he was the opposite. He would procrastinate. He doesn't have very good interaction skills; he doesn't know how to follow up small talk. I think we tried to help each other with our difficulties, but both of us actually got worse which I thought probably wasn't good. He was holding me back in my social and perception skills so we broke up but we have stayed distant friends.

I had one friend who was female, she has autism as well. We couldn't maintain our friendship because as soon as I found other friends at college, she said "we're not friends because you've got another friend". I didn't mean for that to happen. After that, our friendship dissolved a bit which was a real shame. I can be very all or nothing with friends. If one of my friends needs space or they're busy when they didn't plan to be, I can take it personally, so I can see how she might have felt like I was ditching her for someone else. At the time I wasn't used to having more than two friends at a time and usually they were in completely different social circles as well. I suppose it's quite rare to have more than three friends when you have autism. Especially if you have panic attacks - that can sometimes make friendships difficult but people seem to hang in there, so that's good. Maintaining friendships can be very tiring. It's keeping in touch and arranging to re-meet that's the difficult bit. I'm quite compulsive so I've got to plan every hour of the day to keep it predictable. It's quite unhealthy though, so I try to make time between each listed task for preparation and rest. I tend to text people; it's easy to do that because I can think more about what I'm saying without following cues in a face to face chat. I don't find forums very easy to use because I come in half way through conversations so I just end up left out. However, they do help me keep in touch with people I already know.

My friends understand some of my difficulties, like the hyper-sensory bits. Thanks to Hollywood, they can link it with superpowers like supersonic hearing so they can put it in context. When it comes to panic attacks, that's alien to them. When they hear of me hitting myself in the head and other things they say, "you're beating yourself up - how are you not conscious of what you're doing when you do that?". That can be quite difficult to explain but it's easier when they actually see it.

As a woman with autism, do you think there are things which are particularly difficult for you?

I think girls with autism have a tricky time integrating in the normal world because girls are generally more sociable, more into trivial things like fashion and things like that. Those things don't interest me. It makes me stand out a little bit in a very odd way. If someone invited me to go to a loud place like a theme park, I'd decline because I'd much prefer to play chess. I might go along but I do find things like etiquette or reading facial expressions a lot harder and, as girls talk more, I'm expected to engage in that more frequently. I don't mind being in groups but it's very tiring to try and keep up with all of the different hints. Guys with autism don't have to worry about plucked eyebrows. I think some girls look angry or surprised constantly. Eyebrows are absolutely key in a face because if some people have more downturned mouths, you look more at their eyes. If some people have quite narrow or large eyes and that gives them certain expressions, you look at the mouth. Make-up really messes with the face, especially with bright colours and things. It can change the mood of the face, no matter what the conversation or the emotion is.

I find it easiest to cope in groups of four girls or more because I can just take a back seat and be a listener. You've usually got two listeners in a group; one that interjects occasionally and one that doesn't talk at all. Normally if I can't find anyone less shy than me then I don't mind interjecting occasionally but otherwise I'll just sit back and listen because interacting any further than this demands a lot of concentration, confidence and brain energy. I can be left feeling exhausted and disorientated after meeting people for a coffee, so I try to keep outings to just a few hours. I include travelling to and from meeting places in these few hours because this tires me out just the same as having conversations.

What about clothes?

I used to dress as a tomboy, living in a rugby top and combats. I went to all the boy shops when I was younger because I couldn't find anything that wasn't a garish colour or a really weird texture. I still get issues like that but it's not so bad because there are so many different types of clothes. As long as the clothes are loose, sensible colours and a manageable texture and weight, I'm happy to live in certain outfits for days at a time. They must also keep me at a nice temperature (I can feel panicked if I sweat or feel cold because the sensation is too intense and I can't focus on anything else). When I was a girl everything was either plastic or fluffy, so I would get a really horrible sticky texture for shoes and bags or I would struggle to breathe because I could feel the fabric squeaking on the backs of my nails. I couldn't even go near someone who had lip-gloss on because I was reminded of the texture (the scented ones were the worst!). I can look a bit plainer than other girls but because it's quite a frivolous topic for me (clothes and make-up) it doesn't matter. Thankfully I work in the creative industry; as a children's book illustrator I can hide behind my computer and let people look at the work rather than at me.

You mentioned earlier you struggled with an eating disorder, could you tell me more?

When I was 10 I went through a growth spurt. I felt out of control of my growth spurt. In the space of a week I had my first bra, my first spot, I went up two shoe sizes and I gained loads of weight. I was very underweight as a child and then went up to average. When I was 10 I went through a lot of physical changes - I went from underweight to a normal weight but that wasn't the personal average I was used to. It was a huge and rapid change. This terrified me because I wasn't prepared for how it would feel or what my teen and adult figure would look like. Without an end point to reassure me, I panicked, thinking I would never stop growing and get obese. I became very self-conscious, attracting further bullying. As well as this, new social pressures came into play and academic pressure only increased as each term passed. In year 6 everyone was following celebrities. By year 7, everyone wanted to look like celebrities by copying their diets. Everyone just seemed to be a lot more mature than me and wanted to grow up faster. That was a really unhealthy environment. I stopped eating for a few years and developed a full-blown eating disorder which I'm still recovering from. I've written a book about it and done a series on dysmorphia. It really confused my sensory processes because malnutrition generally makes you more anxious and sensitive. For me, that was a very trippy phase of anorexia. I didn't cope very well with that.

Restricted eating takes away the variety; something that's a real challenge to try and maintain now that I live on my own and when I lived on my own at university. Living on bread and apples was an affordable diet, and it was one less complication to have to deal with. The option of not having to maintain variety is very appealing and I still struggle with that today, especially now that I've got so many other interactions and a lot of it is on a professional level, like bills, utilities and the internet. Eating takes a back seat as I try and maintain other things.

I started actively restricting when I was about 13. Now, at 22 my diet is still a little restricted. People didn't know until I was 16; I frequently collapsed in school and college but I just didn't tell anyone. By then I knew that it wasn't right to be collapsing but I assumed if people knew I was fasting daily, they would probably get angry at me. There was something addictive about having the strict routine: eating and ticking off exactly what I had planned, and written down, to eat that day. Much of the time I usually ate a bit over what I had designated for the day. Scarily, after some years of practice, I struggled to eat even half of what my already restricted diet allowed. I still think the monotony feels safer than having variety because there's less information to take in and it's easy to predict. I have friends and family who support me and encourage me to eat more in variety and quantity, but they don't push me over the edge of what I can cope with as badly as the educational psychologist did.

Could you tell me more about your dysmorphia?

I don't know if the dysmorphia causes my eating problems or if it's rooted in the eating problems but the less I ate, the more my face changed from day to day. Not physically, but my perception of it. Some days my nose would look bigger but other days my mouth would look thinner. I think it was worst when I was about 16; I was 6 stone. I would look at my hands and they would actually change. To me they looked like they were physically growing and shrinking between many different sizes within minutes. That was the worst point it got to. Now it normally changes slowly over days. I'll look at myself and think I'm slightly bigger or slightly smaller but I think that's manageable because apparently everyone has fat or thin days. In general, I think that's more based on self-esteem than eating. I still experience dysmorphia most days. I did draw a diary for two weeks and the differences between each picture were huge. It was a really interesting experiment (though at times, a bit shocking). Photographs don't work the same because my perspective changes daily so I cannot even see what my photos really look like! Drawing a flat 2D picture that you've done yourself, you can look back the next day and say "I honestly thought my eyes were that small". It's a very effective way of highlighting how inconsistent my perspective is. It can be therapeutic because I'm drawing the same thing every day. I can always stop if it gets too scary but it's a nice eye opener and a reminder to take my point of view with a pinch of salt.

Thank you for sharing this with us, is there anything else you would like to share?

To help other people with autism and their friends and relatives, here's a glimpse of how I experience day-to-day life:

Area	Difficulty	Coping Mechanism
Eyes	Can't make eye contact.	Look at eyebrows or another facial feature near or around the eye socket area.
Ears	Sound is painful at certain volumes but it affects my entire body, not just my ears. Some sirens, if loud, close and sharp enough can send me into an instant panic attack. I flinch and sometimes get thrown down in the street if an ambulance puts its siren on right next to me (this is not at all voluntary on my body's part).	Earplugs do not help despite reducing the volume slightly. A hat can work, but only if it fits snugly. Trains are also painful but I can put loud music on (with plenty of bass and a predictable rhythm) to drown out the screeching.
Hands	Shaking hands is not something I'm comfortable doing or fully understand why this gesture means "pleased to meet you".	It is a quick process so it is easy to just get it over with and assume a formal friendship, at least for that meeting time, is established.
Eyelashes	I feel them clack together every time I blink. Outdoors and loud situations that involve sharp pitches drown it out but then my ears have to pay.	I don't mind it but recognise non-autistics do not have this experience unless in a very quiet place while blinking.

Area	Difficulty	Coping Mechanism
Mouth	Tastes change with age but the intensity for autistic taste buds doesn't reduce. Textures can make food taste different. I can't eat mashed potato but I love roasted potatoes and chips. Often autistic girls are under a lot of scrutiny when they develop eating disorders. Unavoidable sensory anxiety around food is confused by others but someone with autism cannot explain it because they don't know anything outside being hyper-sensitive.	When eating out, it is simple to ask for some ingredients to be changed or missed out of dishes. Mixing and matching sides works out cheaper and you can customise your own meals.
Nose	Smells are very strong for me. I do not have to be very near to anything to pick up changes in scent. If I'm trying new foods and am uncertain of ingredients, I will come closer to smell before I risk taste (taste being just as pungent as smell and harder to recover from because it involves oral contact).	It can't be helped when a sewer pipe breaks for example. It is useful if drinks are mixed up (for example coke and diet coke etc.). I smell each one slightly differently without drinking any: • Coke is very sweet. • Diet Coke is slightly less sweet than Coke. • Coke Zero is slightly sour. • Pepsi is sweeter than Diet Coke but less sweet than Coke. • Diet Pepsi is less sweet than Pepsi. • Pepsi Max is less sour than Coke Zero and not sweet.
Skin	My skin feels very oily in hot weather, even if it's not visibly noticeable to others.	I just make sure I have something to wipe with. It doesn't actively clean or improve anything, because my skin is not very greasy, but it just reassures me that I'm able to do something psychological to reduce the texture.

Area	Difficulty	Coping Mechanism
Hair	I feel it brush and make noise against me.	Keeping it brushed and conditioned reduces the noise slightly. I need a lot of confidence to tie it back because it exposes my face and invites more attempted eye contact with others.
Neck	Can't wear spiky jewellery on my neck or wrists because I am squeamish about it catching my veins or cutting/snagging my skin. Soft textures by my neck can make me choke.	Wear loose scarves or solid bangles instead.
Fingernails	I cannot wear full gloves of any kind of material except rubber (even then, just in short time periods like 15 minutes at a time). I can feel and hear the texture grating on my finger nails and this makes me grit my teeth and feel sick. Eating wet peas has the same effect because the sound is the same, but against my teeth instead.	Fingerless gloves are a cheap and simple solution. You can cut some gloves you already have. For me, mittens do not feel any nicer, I have to have my nails exposed to air.
Ankles	Many kids with autism stand on their tip toes to avoid a strange and shared belief amongst autistics only, that skin on the back of the ankle will slit if you put your heel on the floor. The skin just doesn't look like it should stretch that much. This belief is not vocally shared or deliberately demonstrated, it is just something that autistic people seem to be born thinking.	Pure experience with gritted teeth normally resolves this hindering superstition but it can be more stubborn to change with some people more so than others.
Skin	Outfits can be heavy or make me sweat too much. Fluffy textures make me choke but filmy or coarse clothing is just as bad. Floaty, light clothes can be annoying too because I feel indecent, but the occasional brush from the garment makes me flinch and I get irritable after just a short time wearing it.	I make a habit of checking both the inside and outside texture and rarely buy some clothes if a changing room is not an option in the shop.

Chapter 6
Emma Woodrow

Whilst ostensibly of mature years, Emma is much the same as she always was, although perhaps with a little more insight, helped by finally receiving an autism diagnosis.

She still likes shiny things and magnets and hates having her photograph taken. She still spends much of her time reading and cannot imagine what life would have been like without hyperlexia, just being dyslexic. She developed an interest in computing long before it was popular to do so which fortuitously enabled her to compensate for other areas of cognition which did not come easily.

She is currently working on postgraduate research.

Different Being

That is me, with my back to the camera, a fairly common response for me. I am ignoring all of the other children. I am ignoring the photographer's request to stand still and look at the camera. The boy on the left has taken it to extremes. He is holding his breath. My brother, on the right of the picture next to me, is making a slight attempt. He is facing more or less forwards but he is still jiggling and eating a lolly and ignoring everyone. Nothing exists for me, except the model electric train running round on a track on the stand. I have been watching it for a while. It looks as though this is a concern for the adults. Even the kids in the background are looking at the camera.

Strangely and unnaturally according to most theories of childhood memory and language development I remember this day well. I am about three and a half. It is just before I was first sent to school. My mother has left my brother in charge of me. He will soon run off on his own and I won't be able to keep up. He complains all the time that I am not like other boys' little sisters.

I have been given some money to spend. I have already had an argument with the man running the bran tub because he says I have to have a girl's toy because I am a girl. I say "I do not like girls' toys I want a boy's toy because they do things and as it is my money I can buy what I want". He still refuses.

The girls' toys are wrapped in pink paper so there is no way I will take one. The boys' toys are wrapped in green paper. I am too annoyed to even spend money on the lollies, even though my brother has. I can watch the train for nothing. If you put money on a station you win more money if the train stops there. If it doesn't you lose your money. I know that the man can stop the train when he likes so I am not putting any money down to lose it. I am keeping it.

I can already read and add up money. I have got my money in my hand, in my pocket, because if I let go my brother will take it and spend it. My mother is nowhere around. She tends to leave me to my own devices - it saves screaming and fighting and so on. I do not like being made to do anything. She doesn't have to make me wear a hat. I don't like the sun in my eyes because it is bright so I am happy to wear hats. It is likely that there was a fight about sandals though but I don't remember one that day.

There has been a dance display by the girls who do ballet lessons. The little ones are about my size. They just stagger about wearing bunny ears and dropping flowers or falling down. Some of them cry; some run out of the ring to their mothers. That is another thing I won't do. Dance. Move where I'm supposed to; not the falling down, I do that a good deal.

My favourite thing is climbing, or digging. Or playing with water. I draw a lot.

My brother has a cat but I want a dog. Every day I ask for a dog but my father is afraid of dogs so doesn't want one. I have a dog's lead. I take that around quite a lot of the time and in the house I often shout at people just as they go to sit down that the dog is on that chair. They believe me for a moment. I cannot see the dog on the lead, it doesn't have a name, is not a boy dog or girl dog. Just the dog I want.

I think my father is probably afraid of animals in general. His brothers have a farm with cows and pigs and chickens but he never goes in the barns or sheds to look at them. I do. I am not allowed to see them being born, although I ask, but am taken to see the new calves and watch their mothers washing them with her dripping tongue, and the sows' new litters. They have a hot light over them to keep them warm and straw to keep them comfortable. One of the sows will let me pat them. We have chickens. I go in with them sometimes because I can open the gate but they are not especially interesting. Ours are white but the ones at the farm are shades of brown.

Because I like the animals I won't eat meat in case it is an animal I've met. My other uncles have sheep a long way away. When I go there I bottle feed the orphans or twins so I won't eat lamb either, even when my mother calls it mutton. I don't mind eating the chickens or eggs though as chickens are not people like other animals are.

My mother said I would like school. My brother said I wouldn't. My brother was right. I hated it. I hated the nuns. They hated me. They caned me every time I moved, every time I picked anything up, because I was left handed. They would hit my knuckle so my hand slammed down into the desk or the back of my knees so I collapsed on the ground. They kept the cane hidden in their robes and whipped it out with a whoosh and a snap.

We were supposed to do stupid things. Draw three sticks and then two more. Only they wouldn't let me because every time I picked up my pencil they caned me again. They wouldn't let me read my own book from home either. They tried to make me read their books but there were not enough words in them to make any sense. "See Jane run", "See Spot run". Spot was a white dog with a brown spot. I still can't read if there are only a few words. I have to see blocks, pages of words to make sense of it.

My brother walked with me to school. Every day he threatened to drop my hat off the bridge onto a train. He has such long arms I can't stop him. One day it falls. It misses the train which was disappointing but even so we can't get it back. My mother doesn't say anything about it. She is used to this sort of thing; me arriving home without some part of my school uniform, or soaking wet from going in the stream, or bleeding and torn from falling off something. All she says is "it's a good thing your Father's not back yet". And takes my clothes to wash and mend.

I stop having to go to school. My brother says I'm the first person he ever heard of getting expelled from school before they were five, but I don't care.

Next term I have to go to the village school. It's not much better but at least they don't cane me. The only problem is I have forgotten how to write because I don't know which hand to use. And I won't use cutlery any more. They say I am 'remedial' and won't let me read books because I don't know the alphabet. They play games in the playground but I don't know the words. I'm good at throwing balls but not catching. I'm good at marbles and win them from the boys but the girls are not supposed to play with the boys. The girls do tricks with balls and skip together and chant skipping songs. I fall over quite a lot. I am always scabby and grubby. I sit on the cloakroom step and play with something shiny from my pocket: a ball bearing or a spring from a clock.

I am ill quite a lot. I'm glad when it means I don't have to go to school or don't have to go into the playground at play time.

I take my own books and sit and read. My teacher says it is my own fault I can't spell because I taught myself to read. If I had waited and let her teach me the proper way I would be able to spell and write. They keep trying to make me write money sums. I say I won't because I know the answer. So they won't let me play with the toys. I don't really care because at home I have a shed full of all the things I like. My father has given me his old typewriter so I make books and have lots of paper to paint pictures. I have the ends of rolls of wall lining paper so I can make long maps or tall pictures. I have collections of things. I call them my museum. We go to museums a lot. The nearest one at the town has a bee hive with windows and little green felt doors to watch the bees and rooms full of tanks with live snakes and lizards. I have some rabbit skulls and bird skulls in my museum. And lots of sea shells and snail shells and butterfly wings and all the springs and cogs I have taken out of clocks.

The head master takes the 'remedial' children to work in the assembly hall. He lets me paint and because my pictures are good he sends them to competitions. But when they win and are shown on television I don't see them because we haven't got a television. They send me book tokens.

By the time I am eight I have read all the books in the children's section of the town library. I manage to get the librarian to let me take adult books. To start with she only lets me take books with pictures on the covers. When I am nine my mother lets me walk to the library by myself. I take everyone's books back and get any I like out. I become very interested in science fiction, especially robots and computers. If the librarian thinks that a book isn't suitable then I stay close behind a woman and pile my books up near hers so I can get them through.

I have grown taller than all the other girls in my school. In fact there is only one boy taller than me. Leslie Peters*. And I am not even in the top class.

Of course I don't pass the exam to go to grammar school. I can only do the pattern questions. I don't know how the letter ones work at all and I still can't spell my own name.

Things are much worse at the next school. At first I try hard and I answer all the questions the teachers ask. I always get them right but I can't write anything down from the blackboard. The teachers throw my exercise books back at me, covered in red crosses and writing I can't read.

One day my parents move while I'm at school. I know they are going. My room is being built so I have to go home to a neighbour further up the road who has a daughter older than me who goes to another school. I walk past my house. It is empty. The gate is shut. There is no-one there. I sleep in a little bunk bed and Charlie*, who used to be a sailor, says to pretend I am on a boat. It is more like being in a cupboard.

The next day in science we are given bar magnets to look at the magnetic field. I love magnets. I have lots that I've taken out of speakers and phone handsets and motors. I have never had a bar magnet before. I take it off to play with.

When I get to school the next morning I am told to go to the headmaster's room. He says that a boy saw me steal the magnet. He is going to phone my father and tell him. It will be on my record now for the rest of my life that I am a thief. In assembly he makes me stand up and tells the school that I am to be sent to Coventry for this crime and not even the teachers are allowed to speak to me for two weeks and I am never to be allowed into the school except for classes or allowed to use the library ever again for as long as I am at the school. Then they sing "And the earth shall be filled with the glory of God as the waters cover the sea". I cannot stop crying. I don't know what to do if I can't go to the library because that is where I go to hide from the others. In History the teacher gives me his handkerchief because I have used mine up and can't stop crying. A girl says "you aren't allowed to talk to her sir because she's a thief". He runs a guitar club at lunch time. I'm not allowed in anymore so I can't go. I liked the club. Only two or three children went and he sung folk songs to us. I can't stop crying. The people I am staying with think I am homesick or miss my parents. I don't say anything. I cry until I sleep and again when I wake up. I don't know what my father is going to say when I see him if the headmaster has phoned him. When it is raining I stand close to the wall to try to stay dry. All the others are indoors so at least no-one is there to hit me.

I start being sick quite a lot. At first it just happens, then I make myself. I am sent to the sick room. I don't stay there. I walk out of school keeping well away from the windows, the long way round past the playing fields. I can get away without anyone taking my bag or putting things in it and telling teachers I've stolen them.

At the end of the year I get sent to a boarding school. It is wonderful to get away from them all. My parents never said anything but then I remember I never gave the school the letter with their new address and phone number. I don't know about on my record because the new school never mentions it. The history teacher here is a woman called Miss Field*. She teaches us about the slave trade. I decide to become a teacher and ask my brother to send for brochures telling me how.

I think I will probably be an Art teacher. Or English.

When I get back to the other school it is just as bad. I run away before the last lesson so I can get to the bus and catch a bus home before anyone else gets there. The pushing and shouting, throwing my bag over the hedge or emptying it into the road. Jostling, tripping, name calling. You know the sort of thing. "Thicko!", "Thief", "Big Head!", "Monkey face!" Being laughed at was even worse. Being ignored, that's what I would have liked.

One day I just left straight after registration. I went to the town but I didn't dare go to the library as they would all know me. I wouldn't know them.

I should explain. I don't recognise people by faces at all. I always thought it was because I didn't look at them but recently I have been told it's more than that, that it's not my fault. I also always thought that of course all children must recognise people (and things and places) by their smell. You do not need to look at people to know them by smell; you can tell they are in the room even if your eyes are shut. I recognise most people by sound. In hospital I could always tell who was coming by the click of their heels on the hard floors. I knew the way each nurse would swish back the curtains. I knew all the patients by their walk too. They didn't even need to speak.

Having a dog is a good thing. I really miss having a dog. If people know you they say hello to the dog and then you know who they are.

Unless I am looking in the mirror I don't even have a clear idea about how I look. It was easier when I had long hair.

So I went to a charity shop and bought some clothes. I put them on in the ladies toilets at the station and caught the train to the nearest large town. I always had some money. I had been saving up my dinner money since the first year because dinner was so awful. The boy who was table monitor would just dump food mixed up on my plate. I won't eat mixed up food. I would eat pudding, so he wouldn't give me any. I realised that no-one noticed if I went to dinner or not. Before I was banned I went to the library. After that I just had to stay out in the rain. Going to a big library in town seemed a good idea as a way to spend the day. I had just started following up the references in the books I read, looking for more books to read but the local library had run out so ordered them for me from the main library so it made sense to start spending my days there. I couldn't get a ticket because the librarian said I needed to bring in evidence. When she didn't have a book I needed she said they would have it in the university library. I asked if I could order those. No. So I walked up to the university. I knew where it was, near the cathedral. I looked like a hippy I suppose in my charity shop clothes and long hair. I was carrying a pile of books. I asked someone the way to the library. She said "Are you new?" I said yes, so she showed me the way.

My first view of a university library was like every Christmas at once. There were rooms just full of journals with places to sit and read them and all the back issues bound into volumes. I didn't know where to start, so many possibilities. Whole floors full of art books, science books of every kind, medical books, physics, and geology. Psychology, child education, sociology.

No-one said a word to me. It was wonderful. I watched the others, the students for a bit then I went back to town and bought a ring folder and paper and pens from Woolworths and went back and spent the day there. I knew about the Dewy Decimal system from my distant days as a library monitor but it wasn't the same here. Similar though, just much longer numbers, with more decimals. Decimals are a problem for me because I have difficult reading them. Like bus numbers.

I realised I had got to make my school let me take O-Levels so I could get into college, so I could become a teacher, so I could be nice to kids and teach them not to bully people and to love books and pictures and science. I spent a few weeks first going to registration, then slipping out and running to the station, getting the train and then spending all day reading at the university library.

Then I went back and went with the kids in the top set to their class and said I had been moved into the O-Level class. If the teacher asked me anything I just answered. I already knew all of the maths syllabus because the school I went to for a year did 'modern maths' and they were just starting. I knew all about Venn diagrams and topology. The maths teacher was delighted. I only had trouble with one teacher. Geography. He was my form master so he knew I wasn't in his set. His class was after registration. He told me to get out. I said I needed geography O-Level to get into college. He said I was thick, I would never get into college, he would never let me take O-Level geography. I stayed in my seat. I said "I have to. You will have to move me if you want me to leave." He threw a book at me. I stayed put. He said he wouldn't pay the exam entrance fee. I said I would pay it myself. After a few weeks of this he gave up. I stayed. He still threw my books at me but now he scribbled comments in red ink all over them. I can't read hand writing so I ignored them. It was physical geography. I was very interested in volcanoes – I had already done a good deal of reading on this. I asked when we were getting to plate tectonics. He told me to "shut up. That isn't even on the A-Level syllabus".

Physics was a problem. Girls were not allowed to do physics. I insisted. I stayed a few weeks. They just drew 'G' clamps and Bunsen burners. I decided that if this had been Marie Curie's teacher we still wouldn't have X-rays so I took myself off to Human Biology (there was no Biology). I already knew all this. We had a few medical books at home. I had read Gray's anatomy and Black's medical dictionary before I was 8.

I had one friend at school. He was very like me, bullied all the time and he stayed in the playground just to get away from the others. He was in my English class in the 5th year when he was publicly denounced in assembly, having been caught in "an indecent act" in the boys cloak room. The next day we heard he killed himself before his parents got home. We were told in assembly not to talk to anyone about it.

I gave up going to school. I stayed away until just before the exams.

My brother told me how to send for back copies of exam papers from examining boards, so that way I didn't need to bother with school I could sit in the university library and imagine answers with plenty of books to check my ideas. So I managed to get into the sixth form college at the Grammar school for A-Levels. It was the train stop before the university so was time saving. I went to the Art classes at school and at the School of Art on Saturdays. Otherwise I just sat in libraries. Some postgraduate students left a notice for student interviewers for their research so I spent a few months doing that. I joined the university Psychology club - no-one asked to see my ID - but then they probably recognised me.

I don't think I will write much about the sex, except to say that girls on the autism spectrum have the opposite problem of boys: how to keep away or get away from men. For me it started when I was about 13. As we lived in the middle of nowhere I had to walk to even get to a bus stop. 1) Always face oncoming cars as it is harder for them and easier for you to run. 2) Wear boys' clothes and keep your hood up. 3) Try to stay in places in town where there are women about. I infiltrated the technical college at this point because I heard there was a judo club there. They didn't ask for ID either.

Amazingly after being turned down by every college I applied to, I was accepted by the best place I could possibly have found. It was in London. It ran on Person Centred principles. I arrived for my interview with my portfolio, stories and essays I had written (typed) and small clay sculptures. They looked at everything with great respect, then the person I later found out was the principal said "Has anyone ever told you that you are dyslexic?" They said that was fine. They would never write on my work with red ink. I was allowed to use a typewriter as long as I learned to spell one word: 'parent'.

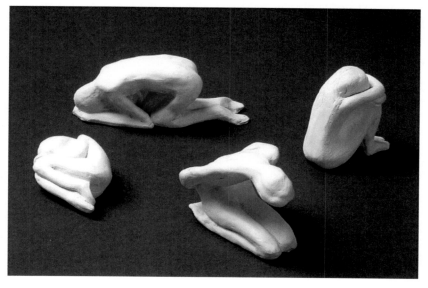

I started in mainstream junior teaching. The deputy head advised me how to hit children without leaving marks. She was the vicar's wife. "Don't slap them, use a ruler over the head, bruises don't show under the hair." I thought I was back in the dark ages, but without the nuns.

I wasn't that sort of teacher. I made my classroom pleasant and full of the sort of things I liked: plants and animals and objects and books and music. I got rid of most of the desks and had rugs and cushions. The next year the headmaster's youngest daughter should have been in my class. So he streamed the school and made an extra class and called them 'remedial'. He put me in charge. I said then if they are 'remedial' I get to decide who stays in the class and it has to be on educational grounds not just because the class teacher thinks they are a trouble maker or because they live over the chip shop.

So that is how I drifted into special needs teaching. I moved on to teaching in special schools, severe special schools, the community, with young offenders and then lecturing and counselling in the prison system. Along the way I got a degree in Psychology and one in English Literature, and a few other qualifications.

I have always had an endless struggle with myself trying to work out if I was intelligent or not, having been told so often that I was stupid. I still didn't think getting a 2:1 in Psychology and a first in Literature was proof enough. I also didn't know how bad I was. I knew I was different but then not as bad as most of the people I have worked with because I have always managed to keep going. I can always talk.

A few years ago someone suggested I should be tested for autism. The doctors refused. They said I had personality disorder, mood disorders and a few other things. They have given me endless different drugs over the years which just made me ill. I have been made to resign from one job after another.

Earlier this year I was finally tested when the university offered to fund it.

I was told "Yes, you are on the autism spectrum. I can't think why no-one has realised. Well yes I can."

Chapter 7
Lana Grant

Lana is 44 years old and was diagnosed with Asperger syndrome when she was 38 years old. This diagnosis came after years of misdiagnoses of depression, post-natal depression and bipolar disorder. Lana's diagnosis came shortly after her son's. During the diagnosis process for her son Lana recognised many similar traits in herself. Lana worked as an inclusion manager in a primary school before deciding that she wanted to specialise in autism. She now works for an outreach team supporting young people on the autism spectrum and their families. Lana specialises in autism and girls and delivers training and keynote talks on this subject.

Pregnancy and motherhood on the spectrum

It was never in my life plan to have children. This was partly down to the fact that my mother had told me how sick she had been when she was expecting me. I had a phobia of being sick! She also described how she had spent four months of her pregnancy in hospital. I had a phobia of hospitals! Even from a young age the thought of my body being taken over by something else made me feel highly anxious. So it was not something I planned on doing. I now have six gorgeous children that are my life. I often look at them now – they are aged 23, 21, 19, 17, 13 and 3 – and I'm amazed that they are mine. I didn't receive my diagnosis of Asperger syndrome until I was 38 years old. By this time I had already had five of my children. It's only with the benefit of the diagnosis that I can reflect on the difficulties I had and understand why I had them.

Pregnancy

My first pregnancy threw me into a complete state of panic. I couldn't quite believe that I had another person growing inside my body. At the beginning of my pregnancy I read everything I could about the changes to my body and the growth stages of the little person in my body. You could say that pregnancy became my special interest. I had a highly anxious time during my pregnancy and spent a lot of time seeking reassurance at the hospital but was often made to feel as though I was just overreacting.

I had always been very thin and picky around food but when I was pregnant I craved chips, bacon and eggs, fried food and I ended up going from six and a half stone to twelve stone! I began to experience sensory issues and developed an obsession with rubber! I used to sit in the chemist waiting for prescriptions and would sniff the hot water bottles that were on the shelves. I chewed elastic bands and loitered around the trainers section in the local shoe shops. This rubber obsession is still with me now.

What is the purpose of a due date? I think you should have a due month, much less specific! When my due date came I sat at home waiting. Nothing happened and I became highly agitated and upset. I paced around the house wondering why nothing was happening. I was like a pacing lion. I couldn't process the fact that what was supposed to happen obviously wasn't going to. By the next day I was very overwrought and rang the labour ward. They asked me to come in, examined me and decided to keep me on the ward. Two days later and still nothing had happened so I was induced. At this point my anxiety was off the scale. I was experiencing huge sensory overload (although I didn't know that's what it was called then) and couldn't understand what was happening but I didn't want to ask anyone in case they thought I was stupid. Once my labour became established I really couldn't handle the pain. I wanted to get away from my body and the feelings that I couldn't control. It was like being at the top of a rollercoaster and knowing there was no way back. My labour was 36 hours long and by the end of it I felt as though I had been through some kind of trauma. I wasn't offered any pain relief at the start of my labour despite experiencing a high level of pain. When I was eventually given some gas and air I was so relieved and wondered why they hadn't given it to me sooner. I was even happier when I realised the face mask was rubber. In fact during all of my labours, the gas and air was the best thing ever. On more than one occasion the midwife and I would be engaged in a tug of war over the face mask. I won every time!

I've blanked out the whole delivery process but I know it involved forceps, mess and confusion. Worse than that was being moved onto a ward - a ward with five other women and their babies in it. I would like to know who invented hospitals - how is it ever a good idea to put sick or recovering people in a room with other sick and recovering people? I kept asking for my curtains to be closed around the bed but felt as though I was being rude because the other women had their curtains open. I felt left out and on the outside as the other women spoke to each other about their babies. I couldn't initiate a conversation with the women on the ward so just felt more and more anxious and isolated. I didn't have a diagnosis at this point; that came nearly twenty years later. With each pregnancy I had similar difficulties. The obsession of being pregnant and watching my body change fascinated me. However, each labour was so hard that with hindsight I wonder how I coped. Looking back, I think that I had read the scenarios of "perfect" labours and I felt that I needed to "get it right". I am a perfectionist! With my fifth child, things went really wrong and after 13 hours of labour I had to have an emergency caesarian section. This caused a lot of problems afterwards with anxiety and depression and a feeling of failure; I was so traumatised at this unexpected outcome to my labour that I decided I wouldn't be having any more children.

Ten years later, at the age of 40, and two years after my diagnosis of Asperger syndrome, I was pregnant again. This pregnancy was my second child with my second husband. When I went to the hospital (different to the one where I had my other five children) I told the consultant that I wanted a caesarean section, but she told me that I couldn't have one. The fact that I had four previous normal deliveries meant that there was every chance that this one would be normal too. I burst into tears and explained about my anxiety and my Asperger's diagnosis. I told her that it was very important for me to be in control. I now knew how my body laboured and I felt certain that this labour would also result in an emergency section. To my relief the consultant agreed with my request. This time I had a very positive experience. Although I was terrified before and during the process, the whole experience was actually calm and controlled. Even better - I had a room to myself (Yay!). Everything was going so well until the staff told me they were moving me to a ward. I got really upset and tried to explain that I had problems with being with other people but they ignored me and I was moved. They only listened when I threatened to discharge myself and began to pull the cannula out of my hand. I explained about my Asperger's, and the midwife told me she had read that in my file but she still didn't make any reasonable adjustments and I was still made to feel like I was just being difficult. In the end I was put in a room on my own and my anxiety levels immediately dropped. Incidents like this have only highlighted to me that so much more awareness is needed about autism and especially autism in females. I can't be the only woman on the spectrum to have had a baby, experiencing these difficulties and made to feel as though I'm just overreacting.

Motherhood

Of course pregnancy and labour is the easy bit. Motherhood, on the other hand, requires you to be sociable. There are so many people you have to engage with as a parent. With the children I had before my diagnosis I spent most of my life feeling as though I was getting it wrong and damaging them in the process. I could meet my children's daily needs; enjoyed the routine of regular mealtimes, bath times and bedtimes; and attempted to be the "perfect" mum. I adored my children and they became the centre of my life. I never struggled with maternal feelings. If anything, I probably over mothered them; I soaked up all their emotions like a sponge. Socially though, I was struggling: I wasn't aware of how to play with my children and even now with my youngest son it's an effort to play. I really have to think about it and remind myself to play with him. Now I have a diagnosis I can accept that I have to be mindful of this, but with my other 5 children the need to play with them never occurred to me. It didn't help that my marriage was not good and I felt as though I was failing in all areas. Bad wife, bad mother and so on. Six months into motherhood, I began to feel as though I was acting my way through my life and my anxiety was at an all-time high. I was diagnosed with post-natal depression and this began twenty years of dealing with mental health practitioners and being misdiagnosed.

My social anxiety meant that I couldn't go to parent and toddler groups. I tried, oh boy did I try. I was given details by health visitors and I had every intention of going until the time came. Then I would feel hot and sick and have palpitations. After my first son was born I went back to work full-time and my mother looked after him. She was the one who went to playgroup with him. When my second child came along my husband persuaded me to give up work and stay at home with the children. I was petrified as I was sure that I wouldn't cope. I did cope but still had periodic episodes of anxiety and depression. My marriage was difficult and my husband could be controlling. My self-esteem was very low and with hindsight I can see how my husband contributed to that by being highly critical and unsupportive. While I was pregnant with my fourth child my husband left. It was an incredibly difficult time for me and the children; now I was a single mother so the responsibility to "get it right" was massive.

Often the children would ask to have friends round to play and I found this difficult. I didn't feel comfortable having people in the house but I didn't know why. I just thought I was weird. As time went on I told the children that they could have a friend round if it was pre-arranged. What I couldn't cope with was when they put me on the spot and came out of school, friend in tow asking if said friend could come round. Even if they asked to go to a friend's house without giving me notice I found that would cause me anxiety. I was certain that these feelings were unique to me and this supported the idea that I was "mad" and "abnormal" – the same words that my ex-husband had constantly called me. When my eldest child was fifteen I had my first breakdown. I had married my second husband by this time and our daughter was five. Looking back I think that my breakdown was from years of trauma from my first marriage. The final straw was the emergency caesarean section I had with my fifth child. While I was in hospital recovering from the section I should have had a room of my own. The hospital was busy and yet again I had to suffer the stress of a ward with other people in it. After a day I discharged myself.

The first signs of my breakdown were that I began to suffer from vertigo and panic attacks that were debilitating. I thought that I was going to die and became obsessed with my health. I was displaying ritualistic behaviours that I hadn't experienced since I was a child. I was told that I was suffering from depression or bipolar disorder and prescribed medication. I saw a plethora of counsellors, none of whom I felt understood my difficulties; I didn't feel depressed and didn't take the medication as I was terrified of side effects. I eventually went to hypnotherapy sessions and these along with the support of my second husband helped me to reduce my panic attacks. I was relatively well over the next three years. I went to work in a resource base at the school my children went to and I began working with children with autism. Around the same time one of my sons was being assessed for Asperger syndrome. I didn't know much about autism spectrum conditions but as my son went through his assessments I began to recognise myself. My son went on to get a diagnosis. At around the same time we had moved, I started a new job and my eldest son went off to university. This was when I had my second breakdown. I couldn't cope with all of those changes. By this time I was tired of myself; I felt useless and unable to cope in the world. I considered taking my own life and I was at rock bottom and felt trapped. Eventually, I received my diagnosis of Asperger syndrome and with that came a huge sense of relief. Now I had answers as to why I had struggled so much through my life: I wasn't weird or rubbish, I just had different brain wiring.

Even with the diagnosis I still struggle with motherhood and life! The difference now is that I don't punish myself for things I find hard. I can make allowances for my feelings and know there are things I find difficult so I put strategies in place to support myself. After I had my sixth and final baby I was invited to a "new mums" group (highly amusing since I'd been having babies for twenty years!). The amazing thing is that I did go – every week for six weeks. Yes I felt anxious and found it hard, but I did it. I also took my little boy to a sensory group, although he hated it because he was hypersensitive to noise, texture and didn't like other children near him. That though may well be another story.

Chapter 8
Wendy Lawson

Psychologist and author Dr Lawson is passionate about the rights of those who so often cannot speak for themselves. Dr Lawson was diagnosed with high functioning autism when she was 42. The parent of four children, one of whom is now an adult on the spectrum, and grandparent to two gorgeous little girls, also on the spectrum, she is committed to creating a world where individuals with autism can thrive in safety and in peace.

'There has never been a better time to be autistic. I am excited with the current technological advances that are helping us connect to and understand the world we all share.'

Autism Spectrum Conditions (ASC), being female, and ageing

Abstract

All too often, Autism Spectrum Conditions (ASC) are thought to belong to a more male dominated population, and little consideration is given to the idea that women are living with ASC and that their experiences are different to those of the men. The following short chapter suggests that women with ASC are equally as common as men and that more consideration needs to be given to this group, especially as they age.

Introduction

It is widely believed that many more females exist who would qualify for a diagnosis of ASC than previously thought (e.g. Attwood, 2007; Lawson, 2011). When we look at the gender ratio, it is more likely to be closer to equal amongst males and females, especially when intelligence quotient (IQ) and developmental quotient (DQ) are factored in (e.g. Fombonne, 2003; Worley, 2011). This means, when we remove some of the obstacles related to IQ and DQ, the gender ratios diminish and males and females look more alike, with regard to their autism, than they might otherwise appear. So, maybe some seemingly eccentric, or very difficult females that may seem odd and so strange, as if they lived in a world of their own, may actually be living with ASC?

Why may ASC be underdiagnosed in females?

Generally we think of women as being more socially inclined than men. Is this true in ASC? It does seem to be, but only for those at the higher end of the spectrum and only those who, if you took ASC away, would naturally be socially inclined in their personality (e.g. Attwood, 2007; Lawson, 2011).

We know that females live longer in the general generic population so what will this mean for autistic women as they age? As far as I know there isn't any research that illustrates this factor, but if you are cognitively challenged, have epilepsy and other health issues, life will throw up extra challenges and you will need more support as you get older.

Females on the autism spectrum may be underdiagnosed for many different reasons. One of those reasons is because if they have obsessive interests (usually a feature of ASC), these are more likely to be socially acceptable rather than the obsessions of males with ASC (e.g. Attwood, 2007; Grandin, 2012; Lawson, 2011). For example, females are more likely to be into reading or animals, which doesn't seem unusual (Lawson, 2006). However, upon close inspection there is often a different intensity about the engagement with our passion than seen in the generic population (Holiday-Willey, 2002). Because often our difficulties are overlooked, not thought of with any real urgency, or not considered to be an issue, our social difficulties may be missed as we get older (Holiday-Willey, 2002).

Another reason females with ASC are not detected is simply due to the bias that exists amongst professionals who believe ASC is predominantly a condition that affects males. Some professionals are not seeing ASC in the females that come to them because they are not looking out for it.

Males with ASC are more likely to respond to their difficulties with anger and aggression, while females are more likely to deal with issues quietly, cultivating extreme "niceness" and perhaps imitating other females' behaviour (Attwood, 2007). Males with ASC may hit out and are more likely to become bullies, while females might instead cling to or over attach to other females (Lawson, 2000; 2005; 2004). A boy who attacks other children is going to get intervention a lot faster than a girl who cries quietly every day. There are a lot of "invisible girls" who are autistic but never get help, because nobody notices ('Sandra': Personal communication, 2012).

Gender, autism and ageing

Although autism in females can have a similar impact to what is seen in males, it may, as suggested above, present quite differently. This means we will need to be prepared to deliver services tailored to the needs of men and of women in a variety of different ways. We should not expect that we can mix this population and expect them to muddle along.

Ten ways ageing females with an ASC differ to ageing males with an ASC

1) We are often said to lack empathy, but, actually I find we are often over empathetic and this means we turn away from situations that require our attention. For example, when a person is sick or needy we may not be able to cope with their demand. Not because we don't care but because their discomfort is overwhelming for us.

2) For ageing women on the autism spectrum our special interests are often not seen as special because they may be commonly found in the general population of women. But, the difference is that our interests dictate and dominate over all else. This can hinder us from being able to switch interests easily. Sometimes our love of animals, music, art, literature and even fashion or certain people can overtake us in ways that cause us to obsess. Men with ASC are equally passionate about the things that interest them but they are more prone to interests in science, numbers, maps, video games, strategy games, engineering and politics. Of course women may share in these passions too, but they may not. Why is this important to know? It's important because as older ASC individuals our passions may stay

stuck in time, they might not age with us.

3) Older females with an ASC might need lots of support and it's expected they will share their concerns with others, as women do. But, being an individual with ASC will mean it's difficult to identify the needs one has, let alone explain and/or explore them with others. Males on the spectrum, however, tend to be more rigid, less social and even less emotional than females, which is what you also see in the typical population. However carers and other support individuals check in with the guys and tell them, rather than ask them, what their needs are. It's a gender difference that easily transfers to the ASC population but it's not one we may recognise, experience or appreciate. Therefore, we may fail to accommodate it.

4) According to some of the research, females with autism, as they age, go through a number of hormonal changes. These can negatively affect their body temperature, their appetite and their ability to cope with change (Lawson, 2011). If those who support us are unaware of these things and if the individual themselves cannot tell you; then either obsessional or behaviour support needs will result. It's very important, therefore, that those supporting us can check in with us concerning these issues. Just because we don't talk, it doesn't mean we don't think. Nor does it mean we cannot communicate our needs to another. But, it does mean those working with us will need to find appropriate communication devices and will need to get to know us individually.

5) Ageing females with an ASC may be totally unaware of the age differences that exist between them and other women. This may also be true for men with an ASC but they may not worry about this. I know I find it very difficult to tell another woman's age and this can mean I'm insecure about how to relate to them. Giving me a way to check this out would be great as well as letting me know what kinds of behaviour go with particular ages.

6) Ageing females with an ASC may have some unusual sensory processing issues, just like males do. However, bigger fluctuations may occur, often going from one extreme to the other. This is also seen within the typical population, but, when added to our obsessive or passionate dispositions we can develop tantrum behaviours that may not have been seen in our younger selves.

7) As younger women we may get very anxious, just like males with an ASC, however our anxiety is rarely physical or disruptive in our younger years. We develop great coping mechanisms as younger females, often turning our anxiety inwards to depression and paranoia. It's as if it just isn't 'lady like' to tantrum! Not having legitimate expression for our anxiety builds up over time and, during menopause in particular, our walls crumble and we can no longer hold it all together.

8) Ageing ASC females who may once have been described as shy, quiet, solitary or loners may

find it very difficult coming to terms with the changes they are experiencing as their physical bodies age. This is true for most of us whether typically or autistically developing. But, if you are a member of the generic population you have access to a variety of materials to help you through this transition. For this reason, you may not live with sensory dysphoria and won't have to battle so hard with not understanding what is happening to you like many with an ASC do.

9) Males with an ASC don't go through menopause but they may face physical differences that impact on sexual libido, muscle tone and loss of head or/and body hair. These changes can be suddenly noticed rather than grow slowly with the individual. Such shock can cause panic and a variety of behaviour support needs that noone understands because they don't realise what that person is going through. Females with ASC will also experience hormonal changes and challenges as they age, but these will be quite different to those faced by males. The commonality is the concept that they may be experienced as "sudden, and therefore very scary".

10) Some other noticeable differences between the genders are just that – gender issues. Some individuals like very 'girly' or feminine pursuits whilst others, even though they are female, may be inclined to less feminine activities. It's the same for the guys. Being male does not always mean you will like beer and football! Whatever your gender, you are an individual and will need others in your life to take the time to get to know you.

The above are generalisations and one must not assume they are always the case for every person. Therefore we must check out each situation and get to know each individual for who they are.

It's interesting to note that some ageing females with ASC think that their autism is more noticeable to others, while males don't seem to have this opinion (Lai, et al 2011). Some research says females tend to have more sensory issues than males (Lawson, 2011), but this does not mean sensory issues are only specific to women with autism. I also know a number of women with ASC who don't seem particularly bothered by sensory dysphoria at all. However, as one ages I tend to think that some sensory issues may increase whilst others might decrease.

This is because as we get older and are not necessarily required to mix in groups with others (no longer at school, college or work) we keep more to ourselves and deal less with noise, people pollution and social demand. So, when we find ourselves back into those types of situations due to health issues or care needs, we are less able to cope.

We often depend on our friends and family to help us with the everyday demand of typical life encounters; everything from budgeting our finances, to getting the shopping done. We often need support with sorting out our personal, educational and leisure time activities, domestic chores, and sometimes even personal hygiene.

I know how dependent I am on my family for many of the things outlined above. As an ageing individual with ASC I can write a book or present a lecture but I have difficulty crossing a road. All the support needs I have place demands on those I live with, and are very wearing on family members - especially when there is no place for respite.

Conclusion

Women with ASC will present and age differently to men with ASC. As women ageing with ASC, we need the social supports that come from human interaction, but more needs to be done. I'm not just talking about a befriending scheme or adopt a granny (although these may be well and good) I'm talking about people becoming educated about ageing with ASC, getting involved with us and being prepared to hang on in there when the going gets tough.

References

Attwood, T. (2007) *The Complete Guide to Asperger's Syndrome*. Philadelphia, PA: Jessica Kingsley Publishers

Fombonne, E. (2003) Epidemiological surveys of autism and other pervasive developmental disorders: An update. *Journal of Autism and Developmental Disorders*, 33, 365–382

Grandin, T. (Ed) (2012) *Different, not less*. USA: Future Horizons

Holiday-Willey, L. (2002) *Pretending to be normal: Living with Aspergers syndrome*. London: Jessica Kingsley

Lai, M-C, Lombardo, M.V., Pasco, G., Ruigrok, A.N.V., Wheelwright, S.J., et al. (2011) A Behavioral Comparison of Male and Female Adults with High Functioning Autism Spectrum Conditions. *Plos ONE* 6(6): e20835.

Lawson, W. (2011) *The passionate mind: How individuals with autism learn*, London: Jessica Kingsley

Lawson, W. (2006) *Friendships the Aspie way* London: Jessica Kingsley

Lawson, W. (2005) *Build your own life*. London: Jessica Kingsley

Lawson, W. (2004) *Sex, sexuality and the autism spectrum* London: Jessica Kingsley

Worley, J. A., Matson, J. L., Mahan, S., Kozlowski, A. M., & Neal, D. (2011) Stability of symptoms of autism spectrum disorders in toddlers: An examination using the Baby and Infant Screen for Children with autism-Part 1 (BISCUIT). *Developmental Neurorehabilitation*, 14, 36-40

Chapter 9

JD Scott

Artist: JD Scott
Title: Listen for the Light
Year: 2010
Media: Spray paint on deep edge canvas 12" x 12"

Quiet Please

I have an old self-portrait
That I made some years ago,
The last of several works of art
I'd stopped when feeling low.

See, sadness, pain and anger
Made me seek a doc or two,
Lo and behold, I soon found
My depression was a clue.

It turned out I'm autistic
With Asperger syndrome, gad!
It was a shock, but sure explained
Why I had felt so bad.

For being hypersensitive
And needing time alone,
For carrying out my loved routines
Or turning off my phone.

I wanted to retreat some place
That's quiet, calm and slow,
The world was way too noisy
But what was I to know.

Well time has passed and I can say
I now appreciate,
What I perceive is based upon
The wiring in my pate.

JD Scott, November 2013

Chapter 10

Zaffy Simone

Diagnosed as being on the autism spectrum at the age of 39, Zaffy Simone lives with Lucy and their cat and dog in Nottinghamshire.

Zaffy has struggled throughout life with sensory, social and learning issues, and has put lots of energy into learning how to manage a very sensitive nervous and sensory system. Zaffy's diagnosis was a relief, 'My diagnosis has been positive and beneficial, it was a final piece of the puzzle for me and my aim now is to help others by raising awareness and understanding of what it means to be on the autism spectrum'.

Art has always been a form of communication for Zaffy. Zaffy uses art and cartoons to show what it is like to be on the spectrum and to increase understanding and acceptance of autistic people.

Zaffy works with a major learning disability provider as a support worker alongside offering private consultation with individuals, families, Local and Education Authorities and care and support providers.

Zaffy cares very deeply about making the world a better place for people on the autism spectrum, breaking down barriers to inclusion and increasing opportunity for participation.

Introduction

You're reading this chapter as part of a book about women and girls on the autism spectrum. You may be a woman on the spectrum yourself, a professional or possibly a family member of an autistic woman or girl and I hope the book is giving you a range of perspectives to broaden and enrich your understanding. I have a confession to make, please bear with me in this because I DO have a perspective to share on being a girl and a woman on the autistic spectrum but I am, actually, a man.

Several studies suggest that gender dysphoria is statistically more prevalent in the autistic community. I wasn't diagnosed as autistic until I was 39 and so I didn't relate my experience of my gender to my autism, but I've always known I operated differently and that my nervous and sensory systems were more sensitive compared to those around me. I also knew that my experience of my body and my gender was different to the expectations that other people had of me.

I was born a boy and fully expected to grow up to be a man. However, throughout my childhood and until relatively recently I lived as and was treated as a girl and then a woman because that is what my body tells people I am. People react and respond to what they see. These reactions and responses shape behaviours and feelings. I behaved and felt feminine as far as I was able to but there was always a sense for me that this wasn't my whole truth.

My story

I was born in Australia as part of a religious community, populated by gentle people sticking to very clear rules about what they believe is appropriate behaviour. My very early years were ideal for me as a person on the spectrum. I was very clear on what to do and what not to do. Much of my religious tutelage was focused on building communication and social skills which was enormously helpful to me. I look back on these years happily; they were years of learning, play and peace.

My gender at this point wasn't an issue. It was not up for debate that I would wear dresses and take part in activities reserved for females; so, exploring where I sat in relation to the gender spectrum wasn't an option for me in my early years. I had no knowledge of transgender issues; I had no reference point for the way I felt off kilter in relation to the expectations coming from all around me that I would be feminine. This aspect of my development had to wait because, as a child, I absorbed the messages I received about gender from my family, community and the media without question.

The peaceful atmosphere of my childhood was shattered when I started school at age six. School made me ill. School was long corridors, full of strange people; school was bright lights, loud noises, confusing expectations and frightening demands. School was too big, too much, too many. I couldn't understand why I needed to be there. It was an assault on my senses; there was constant change, and I was expected to learn things I either already knew about or things that I simply wasn't interested in.

Without a diagnosis, teachers had nothing to connect my disengagement, 'tantrums', aggression and class-clowning to, I was labelled as a problem child and punished for behaviours that were, I now realise, my ways of coping with the assault on my delicate autistic system that school represented.

I was bullied by the other children at school. Children struggle with difference, their greatest fear being that they themselves will be singled out. School can be a case of establishing yourself as a bully before some other bully establishes that you should be bullied. I've never been able to understand why people aren't just authentic and truthful, so mean playground games eluded me completely which left me vulnerable. Additionally, some of the more subtle bullying didn't register with me until years later. I simply didn't appreciate that it was happening at the time. At home, I was always being told that I was unique and special, and so I had a strong sense of my own worth and my right to have a place in the world - this helped enormously. I coped with school; I didn't learn and I didn't engage. It was simply a part of my otherwise happy life that I had to endure and survive.

At age nine, I discovered surfing. Once I'd managed to make it over the sand into the ocean, it became the love of my life and one of my greatest teachers. Sand remains a necessary evil that I navigate with disdain. Surfing however is the reward at the end of the torture and is an absolute pleasure for me. Surfing has taught me many of the philosophies and social skills I have. An important lesson which I am always reminded of whenever I am overwhelmed is that if I stay still, take no action, wait, relax and trust, I will come to the surface of whatever has overwhelmed me. This is an analogy which links to being swallowed up by a wave; something that happens when surfing.

The onset of puberty changed my relationship to my body, my gender, my community and to the wider world. My mother describes this as a time she felt as if she had lost me. I had already discovered that alcohol dulled my nervous system, calming me and helping me to cope with overstimulation. My dad gave me a small beer when I was around 10 years old, it was his way of thanking me for helping him out and meant quite innocently. But for me, it was an introduction to the elixir of calm; the magic potion that would help me to cope when nothing else had worked before. I began stealing it from my parents, and did so until I moved out. The changes in my body and in the way people reacted to me following the development of my breasts and body left me shattered and needing all the 'help' I could get.

Depleted, ill and fearful, I left the religious community in my early twenties. A search for company and the sense of belonging I craved led me to hang out with friends in pubs and bars. It was here that I created some of my most interesting and expressive art. I found that I can cope with loud, busy, sociable atmospheres if I use a sketchbook (sometimes, in desperation, a beer mat or table top!) and with a pencil in each hand, begin tapping and making small marks without looking at the paper. Without planning, without thought, I would channel the atmosphere, conversations, music and my reactions to it all through the pencils onto the paper. Looking back at pictures I drew years ago, I can remember the conversations they represent, the way I felt at the time, and who I was with.

As my twenties progressed, my health deteriorated. I had constant ear infections and bowel problems; I was exhausted but I couldn't sleep; I was clumsy, overwhelmed, I was having lots of seizures and headaches, and my muscles were tense and achy. Seeking support via conventional routes, I was wrongly diagnosed with multiple sclerosis at twenty two. I lived with this diagnosis, knowing in my gut it was wrong and coping in a variety of ways - some healthy, some less so - until I staggered into the presence of an herbalist working exclusively with terminally ill patients. She spent time listening to what I was coping with and told me that when nature was handing out nervous systems, I was holding the door for the others! She told me that I was wired up differently to other people. Her recognition that there was something fundamentally different or unusual about the way my brain related to the environment confirmed my own understanding of myself. From this point, in my late twenties, my life started to turn around.

An elimination diet showed that I was intolerant to gluten (present in many grains such as wheat and oats) and casein (a protein present in cow's dairy products). I have more recently learned that such intolerance is common in autistic people. Cutting these from my diet has made a life enhancing change in my general health and more specifically, my bowel issues are cleared up and I no longer have ear infections. If I slip up or accidently eat gluten or casein, I soon know about it!

Around this time, I also explored other ways to manage my health including cranio-sacral therapy, homeopathy, herbalism, relaxation, meditation, exercise and diet. I continued to draw in busy places as a coping mechanism which helped me to manage social interaction.

So much of my energy had gone into managing my health; I hadn't taken the time to process my relationship to my gender. Following puberty, I had come to terms with my situation and was used to being described or defined by others as a lesbian. I looked like a lesbian in that I appeared to be a woman who was attracted to other women. I also felt at home in the 'gay' scene because all sorts of variations on gender were accepted so I felt I could be known as more than the gender and sexuality labels that had been assigned to me.

In 2002, I secured a place at Southern Cross University, New South Wales, to study a Bachelor's degree in Naturopathy and Complementary Medicine. This was my first step into education since my disastrous experience at school. But, because I loved the subject matter and had been learning about all that the course taught for years to feed my own interest, I was confident that I would enjoy the course. I felt that I had at last found a life path which I could delight in and which would support my interest in health, nutrition and wellbeing.

However, I soon discovered that I had learning issues that I hadn't known about or understood before. I loved learning in lectures, discussing with friends and reading countless books about the subjects we were covering. Yet, when the time came for me to produce essays, to demonstrate my vast knowledge and understanding, I produced gobbledygook!

My lecturers were confused. By talking with me they knew I had a fantastic grasp of the subject, but when they read my work, they cringed; it was as if I had asked a small child to write it for me! Over time, my health began to reflect the impact of the stress I was under. I was doing masses more work than other students. To learn the facts, I would write and re-write chapters of books, staying up throughout the night until I knew my brain had assimilated the information. I would produce essays well in advance and then re-write and tweak them over and over, asking friends and lecturers to explain to me where I'd gone wrong and how to express what I wanted to say differently. Sadly, although I was managing to pass and despite lots of support from baffled tutors, in the end, I became so ill I had to leave the course. I left an indelible marker of my time there in the shape of a sandstone sculpture called 'Healing Hands'.

One day, in my late thirties, I found myself, quite unplanned and uninvited, at a conference. The conference was about autism and a guy called Tony Attwood was speaking at it. I entered the conference, but it was noisy and overwhelming in there so I headed for the outside where I could hear what was being said from a distance that felt ok for me. Listening to Tony telling the audience how autistic people are easily overwhelmed by sensory information, including sound, I started to feel a stirring of association with his words. I then wandered inside toward a book stall, and, always drawn to books, I picked up one with an incredible title that resonated with me enormously. The book, 'Thinking in Pictures' was by Temple Grandin, a world famous autistic woman, and explained how her brain processes words as pictures, allowing her some 'super powers' whilst also causing a degree of difficulty and confusion on occasion. As I leafed through the pages, reading her words and seeing her diagrams, I knew that I was just like her. After the conference, a colleague approached Tony Attwood and he arranged for his team to assess me. I was diagnosed with 'high functioning autism' in 2007. My diagnosis was a relief, a blessing, a door to step through into the rest of my life.

It was around this same time that I began to voice to people who love me that I am a man. Initially, possibly as a result of my autistic literality, I described myself as bi-gendered. This is a condition of relating to one's self as neither and/or both gender. I know I am a woman because my body has woman parts. I know I am a man because that's how I feel inside. This was the beginning for me of a process of understanding my relationship to my gender. I knew it was the right path for me.

Since my autism diagnosis, I have devoted more and more of my time to understanding autism and finding ways to generate awareness, understanding and acceptance of autistic people. In Australia, I set up a company which aimed to bring together autistic artists, putting on exhibitions and promoting their work. I started to produce merchandise promoting autism and raising awareness.

In 2009, I met Dr Wendy Lawson who asked me to illustrate her book, 'The Passionate Mind, how people with autism learn'. Wendy also invited me to join her on a speaking tour of the UK, which I did in early 2012. We visited a range of providers, schools and parent's groups, as well as the University of Birmingham, talking about our own perspectives and experience of being on the autism spectrum, giving advice and information to people who valued this. I decided that I wanted to become an independent autism consultant, supporting autistic people and allowing those who support and love them to gain a better understanding of what it is like to live with autism.

Since then, my dog Beni and I have moved to the UK to be with my partner, Lucy, and I have never been happier. I work part time for a learning disability charity supporting people in their own home to live as independently as they can. One of the people we support is autistic and the support I have given to the staff team to better understand the way that they and the environment affect the person has allowed the person to thrive. Their language has developed and they have felt able to start to take control of their own life. This level of empowerment was simply not available to this person before they were supported by someone who has a thorough understanding and personal experience of autism.

I also work regularly for an alternative education centre called Rainbow Horses. Here, autistic children are supported to better understand themselves and those around them by interacting with horses and other animals. I have also worked with a Local Authority to support young people in care by educating their families and support staff and I have worked with individuals. Alongside this, I continue to talk at conferences, universities, schools and parent groups. Just this week, I was one of the speakers at the National Autistic Society's 'Autism and Participation' Conference. I love my work and I am delighted to be able to make a positive difference to other people's lives.

Since living in the UK, I have sourced support around understanding the issues I have always lived with about my gender identity. Early last year I was referred to a gender clinic and diagnosed with gender dysphoria. This means I am a man but my body is female. This is a medical condition which can be treated. I now define myself as a man and I ask people who know me to say 'he' and 'him' instead of 'she' and 'her' when they talk to and about me.

Reflections on autism

One of the ways I like to describe autism is that it is an operating difference rather than a deficit. My partner uses a laptop with a Windows operating system, whereas I prefer my Macbook. When Lucy tries to use my laptop, she gets confused, frustrated and always needs to ask me to help her to do whatever she is stuck on; "Zaffy, how do I cut and paste?", "come and show me where my work has gone!", "Grrr!! I can't understand your laptop, it doesn't make any sense!!". When I use a Windows PC, I feel the same - it doesn't do what I expect it to do and it seems less responsive.

It seems to me that the world we live in is geared up to meet the needs of people who operate from one kind of system. The people who have a different system have to try to fit in with that or get used to the way they will be overlooked, mistreated, ignored and assumed to be broken or incomplete.

We know that a brand new, very expensive, gorgeous apple computer is capable of doing all sorts of wonderful and amazing things, but in the hands of someone who has only ever used a Windows PC and has no interest in the Apple system, it will seem confusing, slow, mysterious and non-responsive. I can imagine Lucy would declare that it was broken because it would keep doing the 'wrong' thing, the thing her windows computer would do 'right'. However, give me that beautiful Apple Mac, and it becomes a finely tuned instrument of infinite capability in my hands. I will delight at its speed, efficiency and intuitiveness.

The world has so long been run by and for 'neurotypical' people, with a 'neurotypical operating system'. Autistic people have been viewed by them as broken, damaged, deficit, disabled and they have, with this view firmly in place, tried to 'fix' us, to try to change our operating system. I know that with the work of Temple Grandin, Wendy Lawson, myself and other autistic people who tell the world how it really is to be autistic, this will change.

If you would like to contact me, you can email zaffysimone@gmail.com or check out my website at www.zaffy.com.au

Chapter 11
Charlene Kollecker

Charlene is a 33-year old mother of four children, two diagnosed with Autism Spectrum Disorder, one likely to have ASD but not currently diagnosed and the fourth diagnosed with Ehlers-Danlos syndrome. Charlene was diagnosed with Asperger syndrome in May 2013. The battles she went through for her children led to her advising other parents in similar situations. She is now an advocate for special needs families. In February 2012, she appeared on ITV's *This Morning* to tell the story of her experience with her daughter's diagnosis.

Hello my name is Charlene (I like to be called Char). I am 33 years old and married with four amazing children. We reside in the West Midlands. I have Asperger syndrome and I have written this chapter because I feel the need to let other parents with autism know that they are not alone in the day-to-day difficulties that go on within the world that we live in. I hope that in some way this will be of comfort.

My two eldest children Tom* and Sarah* both have diagnoses of Attention Deficit Hyperactivity Disorder (ADHD) and autism, Adam* has Ehlers-Danlos Syndrome (type 3), and Lucy* has Attention Deficit Disorder but also possible Autism Spectrum Disorder (ASD). A while ago I realised that I was just like my kids when I was growing up. Finally it was all beginning to make sense and I felt like I knew who I was as a person (this will all unfold further on during the chapter).

I shall now go on to explain a bit about my life and how I got to where I am at today.

I started my relationship with my first husband, the father of my 2 eldest children when I was 15. I latched on quite early because I just had that need to feel like somebody wanted me. During those years there was a lot of stuff going on and my head was all over the place. I was in and out of jobs and struggled in the marriage, which was an abusive relationship. I left him in 2002 and entered another relationship straight away. I know that was too soon; I know I wasn't ready. There was no love in that marriage but I had two more beautiful children so I don't regret it. I did go through a lot of emotional and verbal abuse. When the police got involved, that's when I decided it was time to end that relationship. I haven't seen him since. He now lives in America, but he does have contact with the children online. I know now that those relationships weren't right and I know they ended for the right reasons, but I also know I didn't fight hard enough. I was too naïve, too trusting, and I didn't always put enough effort in. In the past I cheated in relationships because I was so depressed, I always tried to beat my depression without taking medication and just dealt with it in my own way, but a lot of the time I just put my problems to one side. I now have to deal with all of that and I am having counselling for it. I've been with Brady, my third husband, for seven years and he's the most stable thing that myself and my children have had in our lives.

Upon reflection of my past I can recall being an odd-ball at school. I was often picked on and I didn't have any 'true' friends. I desperately wanted to have friends, but I really struggled initiating and sustaining friendships. My mum left when I was quite young, so I was raised by my dad and my aunt. My aunt was a very positive role model in my life. She kind of was my mum - she taught me everything I know and helped shape the person I am. She was my backbone whilst growing up. Aunt Dee was always there for me and I know that without her I wouldn't be where I am today. I sadly left school without taking any GCSEs. I had to deal with a lot during my childhood, but I really struggled with expressing emotion. I struggled to deal with my mother leaving when I was young and my dad having cancer. I wasn't even able to grieve appropriately for my aunt when she died or for the loss of my stillborn twins.

I started seeing problems with my daughter Sarah when she was two and a half. She was really difficult. She would urinate in her brother's toy box and on the carpets and wipe faeces on the wall. She met all of her milestones at 2, but she regressed a bit when she was two and a half and had to learn most of it again. I tried to get support but social services thought it could be as a result of the emotional situation going on at the time (I was going through a relationship breakdown with my first husband). She was a fussy child and very clingy, she was also very wary of people and extremely anxious. Then again, she could be very loving – almost too loving - and she could sometimes be too trusting. That's something I recognised in myself too when I had my 'shower moment' (I refer to this later on). I was also too trusting. In 2007, early on in my relationship with Brady, she made a false accusation against him which resulted in a social services intervention – Brady had to leave the house for the night. I knew he hadn't done what she had accused him of doing because I had seen how she got the bump on her head. When social services intervened, that's when school staff queried ADHD. She was diagnosed with ADHD three months later. My daughter was struggling in the classroom and they put this down to her ADHD but the strategies they were trialling were not successful. She was also lying and stealing.

Sarah was hitting children in the playground for no reason, this was completely out of character for her. I found out later that she knew that by hitting children in the playground she would be allowed to go to computer club at lunchtime. She would call children inappropriate names and was often excluded within school for an afternoon or a morning. One day I went to school to meet with her teacher and I discovered pens, rubbers, pencil tins and cuddly toys that didn't belong to her hidden in her desk. She had told another child that if they brought in all these things she would be their friend. That's not an appropriate way of making friends. On another occasion while I was waiting outside school, a woman was giving me dirty looks. On confronting her, she hurled abuse at me. Later, she came back and apologised for her behaviour and told me that her son was having difficulties in school; apparently he was feeding off my daughter's behaviour and getting worse. That gutted me. It gutted me that my daughter's behaviour could be affecting another child like that. Things got so bad at that school that we had to move schools again. Each time we moved schools, we had to move the other children. This affected my daughter's relationship with her siblings. At another school, the last one before we moved from Kent up to Staffordshire, a mother confronted me because she thought

I wanted to hit her! My daughter must have been having problems with her son and had told him I would hit his mother. We had a home/school communication book full of incidents like this!

Her ADHD medication didn't work from the start, so, as we thought she was showing signs of autism, we embarked on a long journey to get her diagnosed. She was finally diagnosed with autism in 2010, when she was 9 and a half. We were still in Kent at the time and we were told she wouldn't get a statement of Special Educational Needs (SEN). Within a month of her diagnosis, we had moved up to Staffordshire and soon after that got her SEN statement. She spent a year in mainstream school whilst waiting for her statement. We then moved her to a special school where she is now thriving.

Back in Kent, she used to have meltdowns at home almost every day. She would be rocking and crying on the stairs. During our first few months in Staffordshire, this continued to happen. One night she was having an especially bad meltdown on the stairs. We were there for three hours just trying to find out what was wrong, finally she broke down and told us. I think that was the point that she realised that she could trust us and tell us how she was feeling. She understood that no matter what was going on we would listen. The wall had come down, that was the turning point. Since then, she has been a completely different child. We're not getting any more behaviour reports. We only get praise about the caring, loving, hard-working, dedicated child that she is. All of her behaviour is now historical. Her behaviour has been completely taken off her statement. It's now purely learning, social and emotional, and helping her self-esteem and confidence grow. She, of course, still has autism. She still needs constant reassurance and praise, and she continues to ask a lot of questions to help her understand things. She has to look at a calendar every day to see what's going on as she doesn't like surprises or unpredictability. We are very close now because I no longer see her as a child causing disruption or upsetting her siblings. As a parent I have equal responsibility for all four children and it is heart breaking when a child you love so much is causing so much devastation for the others. Our relationship was quite disgruntled before she was diagnosed. It wasn't because I didn't love her or didn't want her; it was because she was causing so much devastation in our family. It's only in the past 2 years that she's started to rebuild strong relationships with her siblings again.

After the difficulties with my daughter in 2007, we were left to pick up the pieces. At the time none of my children had a diagnosis of autism (just Tom's ADHD). I went through a lot for my daughter: getting solicitor intervention, expert reports proving the need for a statement and specialist provision which resulted in an education tribunal. People began asking me questions and coming to me for advice. I started a closed Facebook group which now has around 5000 members. Sometimes I go on there and give a bit of advice but it is almost running itself now. Around the time Sarah was diagnosed, I started going on courses with the National Autistic Society (NAS). I also joined a support group as a parent wanting advice. In the end I was co-running the group and helping with fundraising. I also became a parent support worker, accessed regular courses and did training in how to create Social Stories™. I'm now a voluntary advocate for special needs families, help statement children and make sure that appropriate provision and support is in place. I also help to ensure that the education setting is appropriate for the child's needs.

My son Tom is quite different to Sarah. He was very busy and lively from a young age. We wouldn't have considered him to have ASD. He was diagnosed with ADHD and his medication managed this. When he was about 11 or 12 we started to notice that there was more to it. He's never had any problems at school, but we noticed he was having problems with friendships and he wasn't maturing like his friends. His friends were all into football and Xbox. He was into Ratatouille and other things. Children sometimes made fun of him for that. He does love the Xbox now. His mind has to be constantly busy, so when he's on the Xbox he'll also be watching something on YouTube like SpongeBob or Mr Bean. Sometimes he'll watch videos of someone who's playing the same game as him. Recently, he's become interested in Minecraft. He plays it, but watches videos about it almost obsessively on YouTube every night and talks a lot about it.

Sarah's interests are very different. She has an obsession with babies. She wants a baby but is so naïve about the responsibilities that come with having one. Tom doesn't know what he wants to do with his life. He doesn't aspire to be anything. He has a very black and white view of the world and can be very argumentative. He finds it difficult to see other people's viewpoints. Sarah is more mature than Tom, even though she's younger and goes to a special school. She has visions, she has plans, she has everything mapped out of what she wants to do. You can have debates with her, talk to her about the news. She often comes home and wants to talk about what's going on in the world. Tom doesn't seem to have the aspirations or global understanding that she does. He just wants to play his games and live his life. I'm trying really hard to prepare him for next year when he'll attend college and get a National Insurance number. I want him to think about what he's going to do with his life but I can't make the decisions for him. I can't map out his life for him. He needs to be in control of his own head.

Lucy has yet to be assessed for autism so it does not seem appropriate to elaborate in detail about her difficulties without a formal diagnosis. However, she is having quite bad meltdowns and outbursts of frustration. She has significant difficulties with social communication, interaction and literal understanding of information. From my experience, if you get a teacher who is not fully in tune with a child's difficulties, it can significantly impede any journey through health services or in securing any education provision needed. It has taken many years to finally get a teacher who is very in tune with my child and will now fully support her in the areas that she needs.

Around a year ago I had what I like to call one of my 'shower moments' (showers are the only time when I get my own space and am able to process and gather my thoughts). My children helped me to realise that I had gone 32 years without knowing who I truly was. I first went to the GP in early 2013 but encountered long waits within the NHS for the assessment.

In March 2013 I was contacted by social services following a safeguarding referral made by a number of professionals where I was accused of Fabricated Illness. My children were placed on child protection plans for 7 weeks and then placed on child in need plans. My diagnosis was privately funded by myself (due to lengthy waits on NHS) as I found myself in a desperate situation where I had to get the diagnosis quickly. I was diagnosed with Asperger syndrome in May 2013. My diagnosis allowed the professionals involved with my family to understand who I was and help them understand me in context as I have a very different communication and parenting style to what you would class as 'normal'.

People with Asperger Syndrome often have average to above average intelligence. We have a very diligent parenting approach and often have the need to understand things fully (usually by putting things into different boxes in our minds) and can ask lots of questions. These traits coupled with our literal understanding of information mean that we can often appear as neurotic or anxious.

In my case I really struggled to understand my son Adam's condition (Ehlers-Danlos) - it was something I had never heard of before. I read reports stating things such as "Adam is unable to balance on one foot", "Adam has poor core stability" and that he has a "significant movement difficulty". It was comments like this which led to me over-compensating and aiding my son in areas which in reality had a limited impact on him. It was my literal interpretation of the written information in reports which was the cause of this, which ultimately led to a safeguarding referral being made. I wasn't diagnosed yet and even though I know I was partly to blame for what happened, I felt I was judged too quickly. Once I was diagnosed, they changed how they dealt with me and everything was much more positive. More was done to support me and my family.

On top of all this, I found out that in meetings, many conversations that had taken place were taken out of context. These conversations were taken in a 'cut and paste fashion' and gave an unclear representation of my communication skills. This really knocked my confidence and made me not only question myself, but also doubt my ability to effectively communicate with professionals.

I am extremely concerned at the amount of parents with Asperger syndrome being accused of Fabricated Illness due to our communication style. I believe we are misunderstood by professionals and by society in general. I feel upset that there is such a lack of awareness surrounding this and I hope that the implementations of the new Adult Autism Strategy will pave the way for a better future and understanding of the autism community. It is clear that not enough is known about autism, in particular the way in which we communicate and the diligent parenting approach that we take. It is vital that these issues are better understood so that we are not placed in the 'Fabricated Illness' category simply because we don't tick any other box.

Since my diagnosis I've made a lot of new friends through social media and I know that I was extremely lucky, because others in similar situations to myself haven't had the same positive outcomes with professionals. There's a lot of misunderstanding out there about parents with autism and it can lead to tragic consequences for their families. I think it's important to raise awareness, not only with the public but with professionals as well. If you have children on the spectrum you will see paediatricians, physiotherapists, occupational therapists and they are all involved in looking after the child and speaking to you as the parent. Quite often you find that when there is a child with autism, at least one of the parents will be on the spectrum as well and this may affect how they interact with professionals. Before my diagnosis, I had some difficult interactions with professionals. But once I got my diagnosis, they understood why I responded the way I did and they were able to support me. I was very lucky that the professionals I was dealing with understood the implications of an autism diagnosis because it completely changed how they worked with me.

I think my diagnosis came just at the right time for me. It's allowed me to engage with services better, it's helped professionals to understand me better and it's also helped me to be a better parent to my children. It's helping me deal with a lot of issues that I've been carrying around since my childhood. I feel like my diagnosis came at the right time. An earlier diagnosis might have helped me as a person but the understanding of autism back then wasn't what it is now. I don't think anything would have changed. It was very new for my generation; even my dad said it was all in my head. It shows how far things have moved on but there's still a lot to do. It's important that I know who I am because I don't want any of my difficulties affecting the way I parent my kids.

My diagnosis has really helped me to understand who I am and made me feel like I fit into society. I grew up thinking I was a horrible person, that I was a horrible friend, that nobody wanted me around. Going through what I went through as a child has driven me to do the best for my kids and to be the best mum I can be. That's why I fought, and continue to fight, so hard for them. I don't want them to struggle like I did growing up.

Sometimes I can be too honest about things. That's my ASD. I don't have a filter. Since my diagnosis I've been working on the way I communicate with professionals. That's hard when you've gone 32 years being one way. I used to give them all the information, not filtering out what is irrelevant. They don't need to know everything so sometimes I could come across as over-the-top. My diagnosis has also helped me to work on my marriage. I don't run away from situations like I did. Instead I deal with them as best I can. We still have problems sometimes and I can't always deal with a situation immediately. I need time to process things. We struggle with that because Brady likes to get a response there and then and I can't always give answers on the spot.

In the past 7 years, Brady has been helping me learn to express my emotions. He's really helped me get my emotions out. I used to be very cold. I didn't show any emotion. I was there for people and I was empathetic towards them, but I couldn't express my emotions or how I felt. My husband is the most stable thing that the kids have had and he's helped me be the better person I am today.

This year I got a counsellor who's been helping me get my emotions out. I've finally been able to grieve for my aunt, and although I haven't grieved for them properly, I've started to grieve for the twins I lost too. There's so much stuff that I haven't been able to get out, that I've been carrying around. I've had to teach myself through going on courses and I know I need to be an example for my children. Ironically I've never had a problem showing emotion and being loving towards my kids, I suppose that's a natural thing a mother has.

It's always been problematic for me showing emotion in relationships. I don't know whether that's my ASD or what I went through in the past. I expect it's about 75% ASD. Since I've started understanding who I am, I've been putting a lot more effort in. I am trying to be more considerate of my husband's needs. I can't expect my children to show emotion if I'm not doing the same. If they're not seeing me hug or be affectionate with their dad, they're not going to think it's appropriate. I find it really difficult and I still struggle with it. It can be difficult for a person with ASD to know how much emotion to show. With no concept of emotion regulation, how do we know if we're being too emotional or not emotional enough?

I don't think you can deny that I am a good mother and my husband is a good stepfather. My kids have everything, they want for nothing. They have a very enriching activity program and are encouraged to do things. Three of my children do Stagecoach, which is singing, dancing and acting. It's good for my daughter Sarah, who's in special school, because she actually gets to be around a small group of children from mainstream schools, so she gets a good mix. It's been helping them all with expression, confidence and their self-esteem. I'm doing all I can to make sure they have those skills.

My son Tom has gone from sitting behind an Xbox to having a small group of friends. He's been to the cinema with them and had pizza. He even brought one of his friends on holiday with us. He ice skates and has professional one-to-one lessons with a coach and he's doing fantastically.

My son Adam (who has Ehlers-Danlos syndrome) is now so strong. He swims 500 metres, he's walked four miles, he doesn't even have to have a wheelchair any more when we go on day trips.

But with all this said, I'm not frightened to ask for help. We've got four children who have a multitude of difficulties. I'm raising them the best I can and trying to raise them as 'neurotypically' as possible. Adam is very neurotypical. He's working way above average in school. He's doing so well. I actually feel quite proud of myself as a person and I'm not going to let anyone take that away from me because I as a mother have fought very hard to get my children to where they are today. I would never stop fighting for my kids, regardless of what people think.

I feel blessed to be on the spectrum. I would much rather be who I am than neurotypical. 'Normal' is boring. I'm quirky, I've got a sense of humour, I'm scatty, I'm silly, I'm everything all in one cup and at the end of the day, that makes me who I am and I'm not going to change. I didn't get any GCSEs but I've been successful. I feel that it's the approach we take at diagnosis which affects our children. I was very blessed with a network of people in the autism community who are positive and proactive. They are good advocates for their children.

There's such a stigma on autism. People think that people with autism are stupid, that they're capable of nothing. The public have such a stereotypical view of the world. If they see a child having a meltdown they think it's a child having a temper tantrum. Parents of children with autism continually think they've got to stay inside. I know so many parents that have been embarrassed to leave the house because they're frightened of what people will say. I used to be that person but I'm not anymore. I know the difficulties that my children have. I will quite happily educate people about my children having autism, but I shouldn't have to. That proves that there's not enough awareness out there as you constantly have to explain to people why your child behaves the way that they do.

My daughter Sarah has sensory processing disorder so when she's out and there is busy traffic or lots of people, she can react unpredictably. I'm very similar. When we go shopping I have to plan every step and if my husband stops to look at some games I have to tell him that we need to go because I don't cope well when I'm in a busy environment. It hurts my head and it hurts my ears. When I'm driving I can't talk to people because I need to concentrate. I have to filter everything out around me to be able to drive. I do get very anxious about what people are thinking. I wonder why they're looking at me. It can be very difficult.

I try to encourage parents to be an advocate for their child, to be proactive. I know that autism isn't a walk in the park and that it can be harder for some parents than others. But autism is a spectrum and everyone has a strength. Carly Fleischmann has really inspired me. I watched her video and cried, not because I was sad but because she is such an amazing girl. Scott James was on the X Factor, he's now a good friend of mine. There are people out there fighting for more positive awareness of autism. Jon and Kim Southall run Autism Aware UK, they're doing a great job raising money for autism. These people either have autism themselves or children with autism. Many people, myself included, have used autism as a strength to do all we can in promoting positive awareness of the condition.

At the moment, at the point of diagnosis there's no signposting to other services - this leaves parents feeling alone. I had to go out and find all the help I could for my children. I went on courses, accessed everything that was available to get more awareness. My life goal is to encourage and enable other parents to be positive after diagnosis and help to signpost them to services so that they don't feel so alone like I did. It is our duty as parents that have already been through the process to become the backbone for those parents who have only just begun the journey themselves. We have to unite together as a community otherwise we can feel very isolated within society.

I am setting up a local support group in Staffordshire with the help of some friends, which will run from April 2014. The desire to help others who feel isolated and unsupported is overwhelming. I just want to help others not have to go through the battles our family did.

We have to work extra hard to be accepted into society. We often have to go out with masks on and fight really hard to cope, it doesn't come overnight and we almost have to become warrior mums. We have to fight as autistic adults to pave the way so that our children and other people's children grow up within a comfortable and accepting world. We have to help them gain the necessary skills to lead them into adulthood. I don't see my children not making anything in their lives because they've got me making sure that they try their hardest and I'll keep pushing them to reach their full potential. I wouldn't change my kids for the world. They're doing great and I love them. Their autism is part of who they are, they're amazing and I'm incredibly proud of them all.

Chapter 12

Lynda Harris

Lynda has been married to Kevin for almost fifteen years. They have been blessed with two beautiful daughters. Hannah* is an energetic, chatty and fun loving "nine and three quarter" year old. She was diagnosed with ASD when she was four years old. She loves music and dancing. She has a large collection of "real pets" ranging from polar bears to penguins. She is always making up stories about them, or drawing them. Danielle* is three years older…almost a teenager. She really enjoys cookery and artwork. Their house is often buzzing with activity and life can be hectic! Although family life is not how Lynda imagined it would be, their home is a place of love and acceptance, where you can really be yourself.

The bangs can be taken out of Christmas crackers!

When my younger daughter was born, we could hardly believe how beautiful she was (and still is!). She looked like one of the babies they use in TV adverts and she had the personality to go with it too - very placid. She would sit for ages in her baby nest, and always seemed so content. We used to joke that we should get her signed up to a model agency! But her birth wasn't easy; I was overdue by 2 weeks when she was born, and was ill with an infection immediately afterwards. We had to stay in hospital for a whole week, which seemed like an eternity. The other problem was that she was difficult to feed. I wasn't, to be honest, very keen on breast feeding but pursued it as it was considered "the best thing to do" for your baby. Hannah* latched on beautifully as a new-born but didn't seem to suckle, and when 24 hours had passed without her settling to feed, I began to panic. I even had a breast feeding counsellor sit with me in hospital. When she couldn't get her to feed either, I felt a sense of relief - it wasn't just my poor parenting skills. The counsellor thought there might be another reason why she wouldn't suckle, and that it was just one of those things. When she suggested that we bottle feed Hannah I was secretly delighted, but went through the motions of being disappointed.

Bottle feeding proved to be equally difficult. We would struggle to get her to take an ounce from a bottle before we had to throw the remainder away. It was a constant cycle of trying to get her to feed, throwing feeds away, sterilising bottles and making up new feeds. At the time we put it down to Hannah having oral thrush when she was born. We even took her back to the hospital, where they observed her for a few hours, said that she was fine, and discharged her. As the weeks went by, each minor goal was a milestone - she drank 2oz, then after a few months 4oz from a bottle! It was sheer grit and determination on our part (particularly my husband!) that meant that she was able to feed. Yet although Hannah had feeding issues, she was a delightful and much-loved child.

Second children have to pretty much slot into family life. I remember telling a friend that our older daughter was lively, but that this daughter was golden, and so placid. My friend wisely said "you wait until she's older!" and she was right. Hannah learnt to walk at around 16 months. Once she was steady on her feet, she learnt how to run - and that was it - the tranquillity had finished. It was about two or three weeks before her second birthday, when I thought the terrible twos had started - daily tantrums over anything and everything. The one that sticks in my mind most was if we were driving anywhere and the traffic lights were on red, she would scream uncontrollably whilst continually banging her head on her car seat "thump, thump, thump." I used to pray when approaching lights that they would stay on green, and tried to avoid being in heavy traffic whenever possible.

Since birth, I took Hannah to a variety of playgroups with her sister Danielle*, who was three. She would run from one side of the room to the other and back again - "shuttle runs" I used to call them. She would run for anything between half an hour to an hour. She was like a human Bulldozer, completely oblivious to anyone or anything in her path. So we used to have to constantly follow her around with cries of "don't tread on that baby's hand!" or "watch that toddler...don't knock him over!" If she wanted something she would just grab it. She would never play with toys on the coloured mats on the floor, she always picked them up and took them to a table. Cars, bricks or anything she had was always played with in the same way: lined up on the table very precisely, and usually sorted by colour. Food was the worst - she was a 'human vacuum cleaner'. At parties she would be under the table eating everything off the floor. Once, we were in a café waiting for food and she went over to a stranger and took all of the cucumber off his plate. Fortunately he was very amiable and let her eat it!

By the time she was three, I was worn out and very much blaming myself for being a poor parent. I remember sitting down in tears with the church playground leader, and all I could say was "there's something wrong, and I don't know what it is." She advised me to take her to see the health visitor. When I arrived at the surgery, I was able to sit down to talk for about one minute, but I spent the rest of my time being distracted by Hannah. First Hannah ran over to a set of cupboards that lined one side of the surgery and found out that they opened. I tried to calmly wander over and stand in front of the doors. She then noticed another set of cupboards on the other side of the surgery, and again I sauntered over and tried to block them. At this point, the health visitor realised that a home visit would be better. Meanwhile Hannah and I shuttled from cupboard to cupboard. Hannah's parting shot as we left was to notice the curtains around the bed in the corner of the room. She twirled around, wrapping them tightly around her body, until the whole lot came crashing down around her! Looking back now it was like a scene from a sitcom, but at the time it was horrendous and once again I went home in tears.

At home, I vaguely remembered the health visitor saying something about Crystal House offering support for children like Hannah, so I rang them. They said "Have you got an appointment? We can't help you without a referral." But I was desperate. So they gave me another number to ring. Looking back, it must have been some sort of social services. I explained how desperately I needed support. He said "There's lots of parent support groups. I don't know about them myself. Are you on the internet? Look them up." I explained we weren't on the internet. So he Googled it, and read me a few names, adding "I don't really know anything about these groups. You will have to contact them to see if they are any good to you." I didn't even bother to write the names down. I don't think I had ever felt so alone.

Fortunately I had an education background, and was teaching at the time. I asked our SENCO what I should do. She said "ask for a referral to Speech and Language...they will refer you on if they think it is autism". Thank goodness for that sound advice. When the health visitor came to visit, he watched her play and asked questions about her milestones. He didn't seem to be too worried. I had had a couple of weeks to think about my strategy if this was to happen so I said "There probably isn't anything to worry about. It's probably me being a fussy mother. But her language is a lot behind compared to my older daughter. So just to be on the safe side, I'd like her referred to Speech and Language, and also to have her hearing checked to make sure that's ok." So the appointments were made, and the wheels were set in motion.

At our first Speech and Language appointment, Hannah wouldn't respond to any toys, much less any questions. She spent her whole time running backwards and forwards along the side of the room. Once again I was in tears, blaming myself and my parenting skills, but the speech therapist was lovely and reassured me that it was nothing I'd done. He wrote in Hannah's notes that she had immaturities in language and social interaction. We were offered a place in a summer school. This was another sitcom moment. The speech therapist had set up two sets of play equipment - one for herself and one for Hannah. This consisted of a doll, plate, cup and spoon. She was going to show me how to encourage Hannah to play. Hannah initially showed no interest in the toys, then after a few minutes she saw the spoon. She spent the remainder of the session banging the door, door handle and different walls and items of furniture with the spoon. And her parting shot this time? She saw the metal frame on the side of the computer, and started to climb up it like a fireman's ladder. I just managed to get her down before she was standing on the computer trolley! This time, and I know this might sound terrible, but I left with a smile on my face, feeling quite smug. It wasn't just me that struggled, but professionals also found her behaviour challenging. The next session was with two Speech and Language Therapists observing her, and it was agreed that a multi-agency meeting would take place to decide if a diagnosis of Autistic Spectrum Disorder was appropriate for Hannah. We had to visit a paediatrician as part of this process, which was interesting. Hannah spent ages getting all of the toys out of the toy box and carefully lining them up along the paediatrician's desk. Then she noticed the taps. The remainder of the session was spent with her running over to the sink and turning the taps on full blast until the junior consultant could turn them off. Good game! The paediatrician wisely decided that Hannah would probably not be willing to be examined, so we left the centre with another piece of the jigsaw towards the multi-agency meeting in place.

I was hoping that support would be in place before Hannah started nursery. Unfortunately, although I referred her in February, she was not diagnosed until a year later. This meant that she started nursery without support. She was still a human dynamo at this stage. She would attempt to escape from the nursery, was obsessed by plugs, switches and sockets, and would climb on tables and say "no climbing on the tables!". I am so thankful that she wasn't excluded, but the Head fast tracked her via the Pupil Allocation Panel so they got emergency funding for one-to-one support. All the staff at the school were wonderful with her. By Christmas, Sandwell Inclusion Support had provided a specialist Learning Support Practitioner (LSP) to put strategies in place to help Hannah, and this lady has become a lifelong friend.

After diagnosis came a roller coaster ride for us as a family as we learnt how autism would affect our daily lives. Once, we were on holiday when Hannah was about four and she went to sleep in the car. I took Danielle into the Guest House - a golden opportunity. We could play a game. That was usually impossible as Hannah would collect all the pieces and run off with them, or just stand on the board! Suddenly my husband carried Hannah in screaming. I later realised she had woken up in the car, and didn't have a clue where she was. He gently put Hannah on the floor. She rolled round manically, her arms flailing in the air. Then she began scratching her face and neck. Soon her scratches started bleeding. Next she started banging her head on the hard flagstone floor. I was sitting on the sofa, so her dad scooped her up and put her on my lap. It's terrible to watch someone self-harm, and we just didn't know how to get her to stop. The answer came unexpectedly: as she flailed around on my lap, she wet herself. The shock of that broke through. She seemed to come round. I quickly whisked her upstairs to change her clothes and she was finally calm.

On another occasion I took the girls to a local wildlife centre. When we got out of the car, Hannah began pulling towards a park which was in the opposite direction. I said, "no, this way" so she threw herself down on the car park floor, screaming. This happened twice. With hindsight, I should have gone to the park, or gone home, but I had promised Danielle that we would go to the wildlife centre. I was exhausted by the time we got across the car park. There was a queue at the admissions desk, so that produced another tantrum. On the way round, she was upset several times because she wanted to go along a different path. That was when I made a major mistake. We were looking through a fence at some animals, and I let go of her hand. Immediately she ran through the door of the Reptile House. I yelled at Danielle, who was seven at the time, to stay where she was. Hannah, like the Artful Dodger, weaved in and out of the crowded Reptile House, disappearing into the crowd. I tried to get through, saying "excuse me" half a dozen times. Thankfully, she had just gone out of the other door and stood there waiting for me, laughing. It had all been a game of chase (still her favourite game!). Then we had to go and find Danielle who, thankfully, was waiting where I had left her. That was the last time I attempted to go on an outing by myself! It also led to me getting a strengthened pushchair via the occupational therapists on the grounds of health and safety.

Six years on

A lot has changed. Hannah is now, as she says, a "nine and three-quarter year old." She is delightful, still full of beans, and always on the go. She is very chatty and thinks she knows everyone. The whole world is her friend, which in itself creates new problems. For example, when we were sledging last year, she went up to a poor bewildered man who was walking his dog and gave him a big bear hug! She plays wonderfully with toys. She sets up scenarios: her toys are all characters with different voices who get involved in long complicated stories (just like Toy Story!). She is able to read and write, and is always writing little notes, stories and drawing her characters. We can now go to a restaurant and eat a meal (at one time she would have a tantrum waiting for food and a second tantrum when the food arrived and it was too hot to eat). Traffic lights don't bother her at all now, and she saw her first firework display this year (with her ear defenders on, of course).

I think the biggest change has been our attitude. In my twenties I would look at a disabled person, and feel pity. Now I see the person, not the disability, and have met some wonderful and inspiring children and their families over the past six years. We have got to know other families through groups like Sandwell Parents for Disabled Children and Autism West Midlands. There is a real community out there, which we are proud to be a part of, and I wouldn't change Hannah for the world. I have realised that every family is different. We don't have to do the same as everyone else. If I'm going to a busy shopping centre, Hannah stays at home with her Dad, as neither of them like really crowded places, and Danielle and I enjoy shopping together. Incidentally, Danielle was diagnosed with Asperger syndrome at the age of 11. She is a high flyer who is doing really well academically, although she needs encouragement sometimes as she worries about things. Hannah is still terrified of things that make sudden loud noises - party poppers, alarms going off, PA feedback, Christmas crackers. But there are ways around this; ear defenders have been fantastic, and the bangs can be taken out of Christmas crackers!

Hannah says: "Some autistic people might like running off. I used to like running off, but not any more. I'm too big. Some little autistic children can be on reins. You might be after somebody's stuff or you might think 'I want everything.'"

Tiger

by Danielle*

Self Portrait

by Hannah*, aged 9

I am good and funny and I like to go in soft play areas. I like my talents because I am really good at them. My talents are running, jumping, leaping even bouncing. I love playing on Super Mario Galaxy 2 or watching my big sister play it.

Michelle the Polar Bear
by Hannah*, aged 9

5 001 years ago Michelle the Polar Bear had 14 babies, but when the 15th one came out all the others were in Year 7.

"Let's call him Catch", said Michelle. 5 years later Catch was in Year 1, and the other Polar Bears were in College. Then Catch was a teenager 8 years later. When Catch was 20 years old all the other Polar Bears were 30 years old.

The other Polar Bears thought:

"Let's buy a Motorbike", and they argued and argued and argued about it for 15 hours. And because they'd been arguing about it for 15 hours, they didn't get the Motorbike because they'd sold out of the best Motorbike. Then the other 14 Polar Bears said:

"Who has got the Motorbike then? Let's find out!" So they went to look all round their house, but they couldn't see the Motorbike anywhere. It wasn't in their house or garage.

"Mmmm", thought Ryan.

"At least we've got a cow", said the others, "But no Motorbike!"

Catch was snoring on the sofa. His clock went off because it was 6 o'clock in the morning. Then one of his Gang said:

"Alright. Who's going in Catch's room?"

Then one of them went in and said:

"We can't do chatting with Catch snoring!"

So they shut his mouth up so he could stop snoring. It didn't work. Catch started snoring again after 5 seconds. They thought:

"Oh no! Not again!" and then they tried to shut his mouth again, but Catch said "Grrr!" and got his sceptre out. He tried to tap them with his sceptre to stop them chatting. Catch woke up and said:

"Out of my room!" then he shut the doors behind him and went back to sleep again. 2 hours later, Catch began to wake up. He had his morning shower and he put on the bathroom bolt. After, he had breakfast. After, he was using his remote control car.

Two days later the 14 Polar Bears said:

"What's this with wheels? Is it the Motorbike?"

"No", said Katie, "It's just a rusty old trophy", and she dropped it on the floor. They said:

"Oh look. I see something with wheels. Is it the Motorbike?"

"No", said Tracy, "It's just an old rusty wheel". She dropped it out of her hands onto the floor the same as Katy.

"Oh. I've found something with wheels"

"Is it the Motorbike?"

"No", said Bowzer, "It's just an old rusty wheelbarrow". He dropped it out of his hand the same as Tracy and Katie.

"Ow. That was my foot!" yelled Katie.

"We're going to plant seeds today", said Catch. He heard bees buzzing and then one of the Polar bears of Catch's Gang said:

"Oh look chocolate."

"You heard the word chocolate. YOU HEARD THE WORD CHOCOLATE", said Catch (in a growling voice.) It was mud and it was the same colour as chocolate as well. Catch went back in his house again, then he started cleaning in his bedroom. He opened up the window to have fresh air. In fact Diego, one of Catch's gang, said in a fast voice:

"Youweren'tsupposedtoeatthatmuchchocolatebecauseitwasn'tchocolateanyway"

"What do you mean?" said Mark.

"You weren't supposed to eat that much chocolate because it wasn't chocolate anyway", said Diego.

"What do you mean? You're still too fast." said Mark.

"I'm not going to say it again. Goodbye." said Diego.

Back to the 14 Polar Bears.

"Awww! We've given up looking for the Motor Bike", said the 7 female Polar Bears.

"Don't give up. We can only do this as a team", said Ryan.

"Awww! We still give up", said the 7 Ladies.

"Shhhh! We're trying to concentrate on watching our Movie", said the 7 ladies.

Ryan said:

"You be quiet, not me!"

Then Tracy said:

"Oh not the 15 hours arguing again!"

"Oh I give up" said Ryan.

"Thank you", said the ladies. So Ryan watched the Movie like the Ladies.

"Whoever's got it I don't know", said Ryan, "That flusky hero might have got it."

He was right. While Ryan was walking back to Catch's house, this happened:

"No, no I haven't got the Motor bike", said Catch.

Ryan said:

"Oh great! I'll never find the Motor Bike unless it's in the garage." So Ryan looked in the garage 2 hours later, but Catch was riding his Motor Bike and the Garage was empty.

"Nooooo Motor Bike! Rrrrrr!" Yelled Ryan angrily, and he stormed off all the way to the 14 Polar Bears house again. The 14 Polar Bears thought they would find out about the Motor Bike, but they never did get to find out because of all the arguing

Chapter 13
Anonymous

My daughter Sita

Sita* is 16 years old and wants to have, and do, what other girls her age want. She is determined she will work with animals, have a home of her own, a husband, many pets, a busy social life, the latest gadgets and have holidays every year travelling around the world. Our life is very different to this, but her hopes are not based on reality.

There were signs that my daughter was different from birth. There were many differences that I noticed, but because of so much else that went on in our home environment (her dad and I separated when she was 5 years old); diagnosis and interventions to support my daughter were delayed.

When she was 6 years old, Sita was diagnosed with dyspraxia. At age 9, she was diagnosed with significant and complex specific learning difficulties, Attention Deficit Disorder (ADD) and Deficits in Attention, Motor control and Perception (DAMP). When she was 11, she was diagnosed with dyslexia and dyscalculia (difficulties with numbers). After several appeals, Sita finally received a Statement of Educational Needs. Sita was diagnosed with Autism Spectrum Disorder (ASD) when she was 12 years old. However, it continues to be a struggle to get the Statement implemented to give Sita what she needs. I have found that there is a real need to train the police, social services and especially judges in family courts on how autism can affect girls.

I had pre-eclampsia in the last 2 months of my pregnancy. I had several ultrasound scans and the doctors were concerned about a decrease in fluid surrounding the baby. I reached full term but the labour was over 14 hours and ended in an emergency caesarean birth because of foetal distress. Sita had a low birth weight (2.2kg) and was supposed to be in special unit but due to lack of space, she remained with me. At birth, she gulped down milk from the bottle, but after that she was not very good at suckling. I tried to breastfeed but she would suckle for a few moments and then stop. I would keep encouraging her but she still wasn't drinking enough. I persevered and stayed in hospital for 10 days to encourage Sita to breastfeed. I supplemented her feeding by giving expressed milk from the bottle, but her feeding difficulties led to her being tube fed in hospital for a period of time. After this she continued to need encouragement to drink milk.

After a few months, she started getting very sick straight after drinking her milk; she would vomit almost all of it back up. She had several bouts of diarrhoea, and she also developed very bad coughs that would last several weeks. She coughed and cried like she was in pain, so I took her to the GP. The health visitor showed me how to give a 'baby massage' which seemed to help. I also changed to soya milk powder which seemed to help with the sickness.

From when Sita began to wean I could see something was different about her. She needed encouragement to chew her food. I would model how to move her mouth to chew and swallow, which she would copy, but it took a long time for her to remember how to do this. Sita did not like to eat so I used to sing songs and give her toys to encourage her to keep eating.

I kept taking Sita to be weighed, and finally the GP referred her to a dietician at Birmingham Children's Hospital and requested blood tests. The dietician put her on supplements, which helped her put on weight and grow.

When I would talk to Sita and play with her, she would respond by looking at me and waving her arms and legs. I noticed that she needed encouragement to reach for objects and play with them. Sita seemed very placid and uninterested until she was shown toys close to her and encouraged to reach and hold them, when she would be cheerful and played. She was also able to talk in clear sentences by the time she was 1.

She started off crawling backwards – lying on her back to get around – before learning to crawl like others and was walking at about 18 months. When she was outdoors she seemed happier and liked to play in the garden and park. She liked stones from the garden even though she had a great variety of toys and books. Swings were her favourite, and even now she likes to go on her swings in the garden after school or on the weekends. Sita used to walk on her tip-toes so her paediatrician referred her for physiotherapy; she kept tripping a lot over nothing but she loved running and kicking a ball. She was diagnosed with dyspraxia when she was 6 years old.

When she played with toys she would get many of them out together. She would insist on mixing her marbles, cars, animals, dolls, beads and Lego all together. If she was told to play with one toy she would get upset and not want to play at all. She was not able to concentrate for long on games and needed a lot of persuasion to keep a game going. She did not like sorting toys, so I would encourage her by making it into games. She still struggles with sorting and organising. She liked books and stories and enjoyed listening to story books on tape whilst playing. She had favourites in books and videos - Astro Farm and The Hungry Caterpillar - which she would watch over and over again, always showing the same interest and joy in them as if she was seeing and hearing them for the first time.

Sita struggled to play with children in the nursery and in the park. She would let go of the climbing frame if a child came near and wouldn't want to go on slides if there were children nearby. When playing with her cousins, she did not know she had to move with them when they moved to play in different rooms. I used to have to accompany her on the slides and climbing frames, holding onto her to reassure her. I also changed my hours at work and spent one day a week supporting her in nursery to facilitate her playing and communicating with one particular child. Sita slowly began to use the role play area to play with a few other children.

Sita liked drawing but couldn't hold pencils properly and kept needing reminders. She still likes drawing - it helps to calm her but she only draws what she wants. Her letters were reversed and upside down. Sometimes she would hold books upside down. I mentioned this at reviews but the school dismissed it saying she's still learning. She could not remember rhymes and stressed different words in rhymes and songs. Despite me teaching her many times, she could not remember the order of letters in the alphabet, numbers 1 to 10, days of the week or seasons, even when she was at junior school.

She liked me reading to her and enjoyed painting and play dough. When she was at junior school she would play with the play dough after school – she seemed to feel better and would become more talkative. I would also encourage her to pretend that we were travelling around on trains, planes or rockets having fun adventures. She would talk, join in and have fun; she was happy playing and had a very good imagination and good vocabulary. With encouragement, Sita could engage in pretend play and enjoyed it.

During these early years, however, her behaviour was also a cause for concern. She was not interacting with children in the nursery and was referred for a Special Needs Assessment when she was 4 years old. At home, she was un-cooperative, easily upset, whiny, easily frustrated and aggressive. We were referred to a child psychologist to understand how our behaviour as parents may be affecting her.

I noticed other differences between Sita and other children in the family. Sita started to complain about clothes scratching her, so I had to cut out labels from clothes and make sure I only bought clothes that felt soft. She couldn't manage going to the toilet easily with a skirt so she wore trousers at school. She would not want to wear any jewellery or embroidered clothes. This became a problem as she got older because we are Indian and so often at family functions we all wear embroidered Indian clothes with jewellery. Sita still checks to see if embroidery or jewellery is going to scratch her.

Sita also used to complain a lot when I combed her hair; I had to be very gentle and often she would get angry with me if she could hear me breathing. She still complains, but less than she used to. She is not able to dry or style her own hair but she likes it when her cousins style it for her.

The most obvious impact that autism has had on Sita is that she has a fear of sudden loud noises such as balloons bursting, poppers and in particular fireworks. Her fear of loud noises began when she was a toddler; her fear of fireworks turned to panic attacks during which she would scream for hours, trying to block out the sounds of distant fireworks. Sita would get angry with me, telling me to go and tell people to stop their fireworks. She would refuse to listen when we told her she was safe in the house, and she used to stay up crying and screaming until the fireworks stopped, which in our area is often past midnight. My family bought her earphones but she would not wear them properly and would insist on putting her fingers in her ears. I used to teach Sita to breathe slowly and I would sit with her, breathing in and out slowly and deeply. This helped, as did chanting "OM" and listening to loud, soothing music. In the last few years Sita has stopped screaming and is calmer during fireworks seasons (October - November during Eid, Diwali, bonfire night and also during New Year's Eve and New Year). My family have been very accepting of Sita and allow her to have her music on and enjoy festivities with her. This has helped her to be less fearful and enabled her to enjoy being with others during her difficult times. It has been very important for Sita and I that my family accept us even though we have difficulties, and we are very lucky that we have the support of my family and friends.

Sita's sense of smell and taste has also led others to misunderstand her; she does not like the smell of incense. As we are Hindus, we have a small temple in the home where we light incense. Often when we go to visit family, Sita does not like it if they have lit incense. When my mum comes to visit or when we visit her she remembers not to light incense while Sita is with us. Sometimes women find it insulting and think that Sita is being disrespectful to our religion and that it is my fault. As part of our religion, women and girls are sometimes invited to take part in a religious ceremony and have special food at a lunch. It is an honour to be invited and nobody refuses to attend. One of the foods served at the special lunch is a type of rice pudding which Sita used to refuse to eat, saying it makes her sick. When Sita was young, she used to pull faces when the food was served and all the women and girls would look disgusted at us, thinking what a terrible mother I was that my daughter was being so disrespectful and uncultured. As Sita has grown up, she now allows the rice pudding to be put on her plate but later tells me to take it off her plate and eat it.

Sita has always found it difficult to communicate with other girls but she has always wanted to, and still wants to, be like other girls. When she was young, Sita played mainly with the boys in the school playground. She enjoyed being active, playing football and running around with the boys in school. Sita used to get upset because she didn't understand why the girls would talk with her one day and then not allow her to be in their group the next. Having to communicate and have friendships with girls felt very unstable and made Sita feel anxious and insecure. She couldn't understand why the girls used to say they would not play with her because she played with boys. Often girls would not invite Sita to their birthday parties because of this and because they found out that she got upset at the sound of balloons bursting and party poppers. Although they would come to her birthday parties the girls did not talk to the boys but Sita was pleased that they came anyway. She would make a lot of effort choosing presents to give them all for coming. Sita often wanted friends to come and play but hardly anyone would come as I do not drive, and most parents had other children and did not make the effort to bring their children round to play. Due to all of these issues, very few children from school came to play with Sita or invited her to their homes. Although my brothers visited with their children and we visited them, they live far away, so we only saw family in the school holidays. I therefore decided to take Sita to several activities where she could still interact with children her age: doing activities which she would enjoy and help her development. I took Sita to Tumble Tots, gymnastics, swimming, drama and tennis classes for several years. Initially, she would walk around the edges of the tennis court and not take her turns during the activities, finding it very difficult to follow instructions. I explained to the instructors that Sita needed to be called by her name and then reminded what to do. Sita would come when they called her by her name and gradually her co-ordination and confidence increased. Sita has appeared on stage in productions in front of several hundred people and continues to progress in tennis skills. Maybe she would never have had the chance to take part in these activities if she did not have difficulties in co-ordination and social interaction. Because Sita had these difficulties, I tried harder to make sure her needs were met. When she was four years old, I changed from working full-time to working part-time and term time to ensure I have the time to support her and have the financial means to meet her needs.

There have been many obstacles in her life. She struggles with learning, memory, concentration and co-ordination. She has severe difficulties with numbers and over-sensitivity to sounds, smells, and touch. She also has difficulties in seeing other people's needs, not feeling remorse when she has hurt people, maintaining friendships, and in predicting, understanding and remembering consequences of her actions. She has problems with anxiety, and controlling her mood and behaviour. She struggles to plan, organise and sequence, and finds it difficult to apply these to her learning and life skills.

More obstacles have presented themselves, which will severely affect her future prospects and emotional and mental wellbeing. Despite having had a Statement of Educational Needs since she was 11 years old and private tutors which I paid for to support my daughter's learning because she was not getting the support described in her Statement, Sita has failed most of her GCSE mock exams and it is very doubtful that she will get the grades to even do a level 2 course in Animal Care. Special school will not accept her as her attainment is not low enough but colleges will only accept her if she improves several grades in a few months. Colleges have also decided to change their Level 3 courses from next year to assessment by exam only; making it impossible for people with Sita's learning styles to succeed. Sita faces a future where her hopes will not be realised because she will have been prevented from reaching her potential.

Sita works hard and remains hopeful despite all of her difficulties. Sita continues to get easily frustrated and aggressive. She can be both verbally and physically violent with me. Sita still wants to be like other girls, but she struggles with maintaining friendships even with support at high school. Sita is vulnerable to being used by girls and boys for different ends. Girls encourage her to engage in activities with boys that she is unsure about. Sita wants to belong to a group so she goes along with what she thinks the group want of her to please them and have them accept her into the group. Although it is not in our culture to eat meat and fish and have boyfriends, Sita does not like it when I talk about why it is important to be ourselves. She does not have the strength to speak up for herself, and I suspect she may be getting into activities which may be putting her in difficult situations. She has been very moody, secretive and aggressive recently. When I have mentioned my concerns to her school, telling them it is having a negative effect on her learning, they have dismissed them and continue to lower their expectations of her. Her desire to be like other girls is causing her behaviour to worsen and is damaging her learning. Sita never says she is sorry when she loses her temper, she struggles with making healthy friendships and does not accept my advice. Sita believes she is always right.

In many ways, Sita wants to join in social activities like other girls. In our culture we have a festival of dance where the community comes together a few days each year to dance. We dress up in traditional Indian clothes and although Sita is still cautious about wearing clothes which have embroidery, she looks forward to getting dressed up with her cousin and dancing with the family. There have been a few times when some women and girls have been critical and teased her because of her co-ordination difficulties, but thankfully her cousin is very supportive and protective of her. She is so accepting of Sita and encourages her to be involved. Sita is lucky her cousin teaches her to ignore the girls and women who are criticising her and to focus on enjoying their time together. We have been very lucky, and I will always be grateful for the family and friends who have accepted, supported and kept us involved with their lives. Many in the community find Sita's differences in behaviour awkward and they feel uncomfortable, so they don't like to include us. I am learning to be grateful for those who do support us and look at the positives. Often it has been people outside our community who have been the most helpful when my family were too far away. I've been helped by many people at the other end of the phone who have been ready to listen and offer support, and I have often benefitted from sympathetic and supportive friends.

Sita's life chances are definitely affected by her lack of academic attainment. She has been in mainstream education and it continues to be a real struggle trying to get the right support for her in school. It was a real battle with several appeals through courts to get a Statement of Educational Needs. However, it has been even harder trying to persuade schools to follow what has been described in her Statement. I had to pay for all of the assessments and reports over 7 years which provided evidence for Sita's difficulties. Despite reports from Child and Adolescent Mental Health Services (CAMHS) psychologists and psychiatrists, it still took a phone call and 2 letters to her school from a CAMHS psychiatrist before they accepted her diagnosis of ASD. Sita has had a Statement since she was 11 years old, but it took a few years to get there and a few more to include anxieties related to ASD. When schools have delayed providing the support written in her Statement, it has caused severe delays in her development and restricted her life chances. Sita has suffered so much anguish and severe distress totally unnecessarily. If only professionals actually worked together (as they are supposed to according to legislation) to help her and our family. By carrying out quality assessments and diagnosing as early as possible, so much of what Sita has had to suffer could have been avoided and she would now be reaching her potential. I often feel that I have failed to do the basics that a mother should do to protect her child and enable her to reach her potential so that she can have the best possible chance in life.

Sita's anger and learning difficulties are impacting on her future choices more than she will accept. There are many things in her life that are limiting her because of her difficulties, but I can see that there is still much that Sita can do with her life and how she relates to her environment and people. Sita gets on well with small children and animals. She enjoyed her work experience at an infant school and at an animal care centre. Unlike most people her age, Sita knows what she wants to do in her life – she wants to work with animals. She has always been at ease with animals and loves anything to do with them. She volunteered to do work experience at Solihull College in the Animal Care Centre during her summer holidays. The thought of going to college to study on the Animal Care course has been a great motivation. She works hard but it is unlikely that she will get the C grades needed as she has failed most of her mock GCSE exams.

She looks forward to a future where she will have a place of her own, pets and a job working with animals. It is great that she can remain hopeful for the future. Maybe it is just as well that Sita cannot see into the future and imagine the consequences of failing her GCSEs. I am filled with fear and worry for her future. I have learnt that the more stubborn she gets, the more flexible I have to be so that I can respond in the way she needs to support her. How to lessen that support is a concern to me. She is vulnerable and needs support to feel safe because she has had very frightening times. She still cannot cross the road, travel independently, work unsupervised, maintain friendships and manage to look after herself. I know I cannot be there for her all of her life and she needs to be more independent. Sita talks about family members getting engaged and having a place of their own and having the life she wants. She says she is 16 and can do what she wants. There is nothing more that I can wish for her than she will be able to do what she wants. But I know that her dreams may not match up to reality. I have to be calm and bring her up to be strong and adaptable – but she doesn't learn from example and she forgets – so there will be more challenging times for us ahead. My mum always says I have to do what is loving and right for Sita and not think of the rewards, because God decides those. Sita has given me many opportunities to show her my love, my understanding and to do what is right, even though it has been very difficult. So I count myself luckier than other mums because Sita gives me the chance to grow more loving. It makes the pain of seeing her struggles and difficulties with family life a little more bearable. I have learnt from Sita to treat each day as new and be hopeful.

Artwork by Sita*

Chapter 14
Stephanie Sjoberg

Stephanie is 27 years old with suspected Pathological Demand Avoidance. In part due to her demand avoidance, she has never been officially diagnosed, and therefore receives no support. She currently lives alone in Cambridge with her two dogs.

Could you start by telling me a bit about your childhood?

I had a difficult childhood. I was diagnosed with Attention Deficit Hyperactivity Disorder (ADHD) when I was 7 and suffered from childhood epilepsy. My mum always knew that there could be more to my ADHD and I could be quite violent; I would scratch, bite and kick. I didn't mean to hurt my mum but I just didn't know how to express myself. My mum was called a bad parent and that it was her problem, and my dad wasn't around so it was just her. She also had depression, and everything that I did was put down to her not being a good enough mother when there was actually a problem with the child. I really struggled and I didn't know how to cope with myself; there was a lot of anger and frustration and I'd throw all sorts of things like my toys. They'd go out of the window and I would go out and kick them around. When I was 9 or 10, my mum couldn't cope any more and I was taken away from her for a few days and put in a foster home. My mum didn't want me in a foster home, but she just couldn't cope - she needed help. So they had a meeting and decided that I should be sent to an all-girls boarding school. Initially I only saw my mum at half term and every other weekend. After a couple of years the school I went to was shut down and I had to move to a mixed school in Norfolk, but there were very few girls. At that point I became a weekly boarder and went home every weekend.

How did you find mainstream school?

I was bullied horrendously at school but not in the way you would expect. They knew that if they pressed the right buttons they could watch some very entertaining shows of a girl exploding; throwing chairs and tipping tables. They wouldn't get into trouble because I was the one throwing the chairs and tipping the tables. That's how I was picked on: winding up the crazy girl. I got in a lot of trouble all the time and I was always told I was in the wrong: that I was doing the wrong thing, saying the wrong thing, behaving the wrong way.

Was there anything in particular that bothered you at school?

At school I wasn't really my age. When I was a teenager I wasn't mentally a teenager, I was still 12 years old or something. I wasn't comfortable being treated the way teenagers are treated. Adults would see you as a sexual person even if you weren't. A member of staff once called me a whore because I said something I had no understanding of. I heard it one day and repeated it but I didn't know what it meant. I was very confused. The other girls were a lot more sexual than I was. My body had hormones and I had boyfriends who I kissed, but I never wanted more than that. I knew I wasn't ready and I refused to go any further. I think that confused people because that wasn't how they expected me to be acting. I didn't lose my virginity until I was 22. That was when I was ready. I knew I was ready and

I've always listened to my body, I've never ignored it. It was difficult growing up because they were always treating you like you were going around sleeping with everyone and I had no experience of that. I think that affects how I see the world today. I'm not uncomfortable with sex; I can talk about it and I find it a natural thing, it's not a problem for me but I view it as something that I don't want to do with just anyone. I have trouble trusting people. I also don't go around talking about it afterwards to everybody. It's something you share with somebody; you don't need to go around telling everyone else.

Were your teachers supportive?

No, my teachers were never particularly understanding. Even in the boarding school, where the teachers are supposed to be there to look after kids with special needs. I felt like they didn't know what they were doing. They were just there and they knew these kids were different but all they wanted to do was mould them or contain them. There was no acceptance or understanding. We were just told we were wrong and that we had to be somewhere else because of that. We weren't meant to be in society, we can't cope with society, we had to be there and do what we're told.

How did you do academically?

The school was more focussed on maintaining you rather than teaching you how to maintain yourself. They weren't really interested in our education. We lost a lot of classes as well, like Geography, and teachers kept on leaving - it was mayhem. We didn't care though; we just sat around and threw books. So when I took my GCSEs, I didn't get the grades.

On top of everything else, at 15 I was diagnosed with **ME** which put me in a wheelchair for a while. After my GCSEs I went back to Cambridge and went to college briefly. Unfortunately my ME prevented me from doing the hours they wanted me to do so they told me I had to leave.

> **ME (myalgic encephalomyelitis)**
> also known as chronic fatigue syndrome – is an extremely debilitating condition which is characterised by persistent fatigue which is not due to exertion and not significantly relieved by rest.

What did you do when you left college?

After I left college we moved to Darlington for 6 years. I didn't do a lot there, I just hid away from the world mostly but I did get to know my dad in that time period as well. He's American. It was in Darlington, when I was 18, that it was suggested that I might have **Pathological Demand Avoidance Syndrome (PDA)**. I was never properly diagnosed because when it was suggested I completely avoided the situation and refused help. I didn't want to be labelled any more. I'd had enough. At the time I was very ill so I gave up and ended up hiding in my room for 6 or 7 years not doing anything. It's only been in the last couple of years that things have changed a little. We looked up PDA and found that it described me to a tee. Everything that was listed there was what I went through and what I still struggle with. I think it would be useful for me to have an official diagnosis, mainly because then it would be on paper and I could show it to official people. Otherwise I have no proof; it's just me saying I have it. That's the only reason I would need it.

Pathological Demand Avoidance syndrome is a condition associated with autism where a person will resist the ordinary demands of every day life. To do this they may employ skilful strategies and be socially manipulative.

Do you get any support?

At the moment there's nowhere for me to go to get support for my PDA. You tend to get support if you're on the extreme end of the spectrum, but if you're not then you don't have anywhere to go. There are also still people that say that PDA doesn't exist. We tried to get support from several places but one of them said that my IQ was too high. I thought that was pretty stupid because I still needed support, even though I have a high IQ. But I do have my mum and she's quite supportive.

I recently joined a PDA support group on Facebook. The woman who runs it has PDA as well and is writing a book. I'm meeting her soon to talk. Parents can join the group as well as people who have it and have grown up with it. It's for adults but she doesn't discriminate. If you need support you can come in and find out how people cope with it and how to help their children. It's impersonal but it's also there if you need anything. It's not in your face or anything like that.

Did you do any of your own research?

I did a little bit of research on PDA. It can be helpful but a lot of it is just explaining the symptoms. It's a bit like sitting a woman down and saying "ok so then you grew boobs and your body changed in this way and then you had a period". It doesn't give you any more information than what you already knew. It doesn't tell you how to cope, it just lists things that I know I experienced. There's nothing really out there that suggests ways to cope. Mostly, the support for PDA is aimed at people who are supporters: "your child will experience this and this. The best way to care for your child right now is by doing this and this" But the information doesn't tell the child how to cope, it tells the parents how to cope with the child. I think that's something that needs to change because just coping with your child is not going to help. You need to teach the parent how they can teach their child how to cope for themselves.

I think I have a pretty good understanding of how to cope with myself. I don't always know where a feeling comes from or understand why I can't cope. Sometimes I do get overwhelmed but now I've had years of practice and I don't get angry like I used to anymore. I know people say it's unhealthy, that I should express myself and be angry sometimes, but I'm not normal so this is how I cope. Maybe it's not the healthiest way but it's the only way I can. I have to do things like shut myself away from the whole world. Sometimes it's for a week, sometimes it's for longer. I can't deal with other people's problems, I can't deal with any external stuff at all; I just have to shut down otherwise I can't cope. I spoke to the woman who runs the support group and she's the same as I am. We both wish there was an easier way to cope but there isn't.

I struggle a lot with food. It's a massive daily struggle deciding what to eat and making it. I can't deal with it, so my mum has to make meals because I would rather have food put in front of me than try to decide for myself. I will go without it; I will starve myself because I can't cope with the situation. Sometimes I need to get away from life. Holidays are really good for me because you remove yourself from the everyday and then you're ok, but I don't have any money. I'm on benefits. I barely leave my house, so I need the holiday but I can't have it. My dad's been able to pay for me to come and visit him in America a few times which has been nice. I reached out to him because I wanted to get to know him. My dad's weird, just like me. Nobody understands him but me. Our relationship isn't perfect. If we spend too much time together we want to kill each other but we love each other and I think we have a better relationship than a lot of fathers have with their children.

What do you do these days? Do you work? Do you go to college?

These days I go to college once or twice a week for about an hour or two. I'm trying to get my adult maths because I failed all my GCSEs when I was at school. I thought I might as well get my adult maths because one day maybe I will actually be able to work. If that day comes I'll need the grades. I did a bit of Japanese for fun too, but that's all I really do.

I can't really work at the moment, not just because of the ME, but the PDA also makes it difficult to work in a normal situation. I would need something very different from what's offered for everybody around. It needs to be structured in a very certain way and that's not available to anyone really. I did some work experience when I was at school but I've never had a job. There's not really much point in me looking for work because I wouldn't be able to do it. I've done a bit of voluntary work, an hour a week here and there which is fine and I can do that, but I wouldn't be able to work 30 hours a week.

Could you tell me a bit about friendships and relationships?

I'm alone most of the time. I do have friends but they have their own lives and jobs. My mum is very disabled now. She has conditions and she's in a wheelchair. We see each other every day but it is very difficult to be together all the time because we both need certain things and what she needs may not be what I need. I find it difficult to reach out sometimes but I try to make time for people at least once a week if they're available. Beth* has been my friend for 20 years. She was also my only friend for a time. I didn't really have any other friends until I went to boarding school. I did have what you could call friends as a kid but I was always really difficult to be around so they didn't want to be around me. I often lost friends. I'd make them and then lose them. Beth has just stuck by me. I'd be lost without her and I don't know what I'd do. Beth might come over once a week, and Tim*, he has Asperger's, might also come round. But they have to be very careful because of my ME. I can't do much more than a few hours a week with a couple of friends. I know that's not much when you think about how many hours there are in a week. They do their best because they love me and they want to see me and spend time with me. I want to see them too, but we are all aware that things are limited by what I can do and what they can give. They give me their best and I appreciate that. I can't really ask for more.

I get along with boys but they're really hard to be friends with because they always want more when I don't. I'm more at ease with girls because they really love me and they're not just trying to get in bed with me so tend to stick around longer. When men approach me they're thinking "oh she's hot, I might go ask her out". They're quite thrown off by the fact that, although I'm a woman, I don't conform to the norm - I'm not what they're expecting. I think it could be quite similar for men with autism, in that there are expectations of them which they may not conform to either. We're very blunt, we say what we think, and we do things on impulse rather than hold back as society would expect us to. I think in some cases society tries to accept people with autism, but it's very hard for us to integrate ourselves in certain situations like work and social gatherings; it's unknown and there is nothing in place to help people with autism in those situations.

My friends know about my condition. I don't know whether they always understand, but I'll explain to them if there's something they don't get. I have a few friends from boarding school and they're all kids with their own special needs who understand that things aren't always straightforward. They live in all kinds of places so we don't see each other very often.

I was in a relationship, but he didn't really understand me. He tried, but he would say things like "you're more normal than you think". It wasn't particularly helpful because situations would come up where he wouldn't understand why I didn't get what he was saying to me. We would get into all sorts of arguments.

I enjoy online relationships to an extent because it's so easy to reach out and not be on your own.

But there's nothing like having someone physically there supporting you and being there if you need a hug or something. I don't think I could pick between online or physical relationships because they're both crucial, they've both helped me. I don't know what I'd do without my online friends because I was so isolated for so long. They were all I had. But I would also never trade them for my real friends because it's a whole different experience.

What are the challenges of going out to meet with people?

I don't struggle going out to meet people but I do struggle with some of the situations around it. In the shop we went into[1] there were too many people, too many smells, too many sounds, too many bodies. I was overheating. Out here, with people walking past, it's ok as long as there aren't any sirens going by or people on their stupid motorbikes. Otherwise I'm not bothered, I can people watch. I don't really care what people think of me if I'm not going to see them again. I can meet people once, have a chat with them and it doesn't bother me because I'm not going to see them again. I get more nervous when I know that there's going to be more interactions with that person. I start hoping I don't freak them out too much and that I come off ok. I can take a while to trust people, especially men - it can take at least a year before I'm comfortable with a man. I'm a lot more comfortable around women.

What are your interests?

I'm good at computers. I know how to fix computers. I'm also good at finding things on the internet. My mum has me on the case 24/7, if there's something she can't find she comes to me. I have two dogs. They're my life. I don't know if I'm good at that, but I think I'm better than the average person who doesn't know how to train their dog, though I'm not as good as my mum because she's a professional. I love the geeky side of things; I love video games and comics and Japanese animation and movies. In my spare time I just like to enjoy all the stuff that I love. Sometimes the ME is limiting because I don't have the energy to always do things. I'm either asleep or ill and it sucks but when I can do things, that's what I do.

What do you see for yourself in the future?

There were always things that I wanted to be able to do and achieve but I don't see them as being a possibility. I don't really see anything for me in the future. I do try and stay positive and think "you never know what's going to happen or what's around the corner". But looking ahead I can't really see anything changing. The way the government is working at the moment, they're taking away as much support as possible from what we already have. I don't know if I'm ever going to be well, if I'm ever going to be able to have a relationship or if I'm ever going to have kids.

---

[1] When we met for the interview, Stephanie and I first went into a shop to pick up some lunch. We then sat outside on a bench for the interview

Can you tell me a bit about your sensory issues?

I'm half deaf on one side because I have a perforated ear drum but I'm very sensitive to a certain pitch. High pitched noises are bad, like sirens. Anything on a certain frequency is very painful. Certain dog barks as well, we had a Cavalier King Charles Spaniel called Sassy and she had the frequency I couldn't stand. Now I've got a little Chihuahua who can bark lower than Sassy could. There are certain songs I can't listen to, I can't tell you what bit of the song but I know what songs I can't stand.

I also can't stand certain smells. They're so strong to the point where I can throw up. I have a really strong gag reflex.

I'm very sensitive to touch. I have very sensitive skin. I don't like being touched sometimes because I can't stand it and I can't stand my clothes being on my body. I have to wear very certain fabrics otherwise I can't be anywhere near certain clothes. I recently had to change my bed sheets because I couldn't stand the fabric.

I can taste the difference if a shop has taken a piece of food and moved it to another part of the shop, I can taste the difference in the air. I'll know if you've cooked something in a certain way, which bit you've cooked first and which you've cooked second and if you've switched it round.

Words from my Mother
Philippa Sjoberg

I feel very sad when I look back at Steph's childhood - sad that she suffered, sad that our relationship was not all it could be, sad that she is still paying for it now.

If I could go back and change anything it would be that I were strong enough to trust myself and what I saw and heard from Steph, rather than listening to those who were the 'experts'.

This world that we live in is very judgmental and harsh on those who don't quite fit in with the majority - Steph was a little girl who was trying desperately to make sense of her world, to cope with her environment and peers. People did not look for how to help her with this; they just judged her as a naughty, manipulative liar who needed to be controlled and disciplined both by adults and medication. I wish I had had the courage to take her out of the school system and home school her so that the school system wasn't able to damage her the way they did. I would have been able to teach her more about life itself rather than her just learning that she wasn't 'acceptable'.

I also feel immense pride at how Steph has managed to hold onto her inner core, despite how she has been treated. She struggles to understand people and her relationship to them. She struggles daily with her sensitivities, her anxieties and her need to control everything around her, but each day she takes up the challenge. She maintains her awesome sense of humour, and is loyal and loving to those who are privileged enough to be in her life.

It is difficult to contemplate what the future holds for Steph - she has to battle the fatigue and consequences of having ME, and the PDA exacerbates the fatigue. She is unable to work, and relationships can cause much trauma as she struggles to understand the world in which other people live. I hope that she will find her place in the world where she can be happy and loved and treated as the valuable person she is: where differences can be celebrated and encouraged so that she can settle into being herself rather than having to try so hard to fit into this present world.

Chapter 15

Robyn Steward

Robyn Steward was born in 1986. She is a trainer for professionals, has worked as a mentor for people on the autistic spectrum and also consults for services. She is an NAS (National Autistic Society) ambassador and works both nationally and locally to ensure people on the autistic spectrum get the support they need. Robyn has spoken internationally in the USA, Australia, Spain, Denmark and Portugal. She is the author of "The Independent Woman's Handbook for Super Safe Living on the Autistic Spectrum" published by Jessica Kingsley publishers. Her website address is www.robynsteward.com

Understanding Abuse

This chapter is divided into short sections; you can read the sections on their own or as part of the whole chapter. This chapter is not written to scare you; many people live their lives without experiencing abuse. However, there are many others who do experience abuse and this chapter is for them.

Why I chose understanding abuse for this chapter's topic

People on the autistic spectrum are often vulnerable due to difficulties understanding other people's perspective and intentions (theory of mind). Women and girls on the spectrum often hide their difficulties by copying others but often lack social understanding. It is for these reasons and many more that people on the spectrum can experience abuse. I chose this topic as someone who has had some personal experience because I felt I had useful information to share. This chapter is written from my own personal experience and those of people whom I have met. I am not assuming everyone's experience will be exactly the same or that the suggestions within this chapter will work for everyone.

Sexuality

There are many types of sexuality. Whatever your sexuality, it is OK to feel that way. Many other people do too. Below is a list of some sexuality types:

- Asexual – to not be interested in a romantic or sexual relationship.
- Homosexual/gay – to feel romantically or sexually attracted to people who are the same gender as you.
- Lesbian – a female who is romantically or sexually attracted to other women (some women prefer the term gay).
- Straight/heterosexual – a person who is romantically or sexually attracted to someone of a different gender to themselves.
- Queer – an alternative name for not being heterosexual (some people like to use the word queer, others find it offensive).
- Gender queer – to not feel male or female or to feel that neither male nor female describes your gender.
- Transgender – a person who feels that they have been born into the wrong gender body, for example they are physically female but feel they should be male.

Types of abuse

Below are summaries of some types of abuse:

Sexual - includes unwanted touching in sexual areas of your body i.e. erogenous zones such as inner thighs, breasts, bottom, genitals. It can also include someone trying to kiss you with the intention of having sex with you, sexually arousing themselves, or someone exposing themselves (showing their genitals when you do not want them to). Sexual abuse also includes **rape**. This is when someone penetrates your vagina, mouth or anus when you have not given consent for them to penetrate you.

Financial - is when someone takes control of your money without your consent when you have capacity (ability to understand and manage/ be in control of your money yourself). Or, when they do have permission to manage your money, they abuse their position by spending your money on things to benefit themselves and not you. Someone might make you feel bad emotionally unless you give them money - this would also be considered abusive.

Neglect - is when someone responsible for caring for you denies or takes away access to the things that meet your basic needs e.g. food, water, warmth, sleep, toilet etc.

Emotional/psychological - is when a person deliberately upsets you or makes you feel bad. They could do this verbally, for example by calling you names, or they could manipulate you, by acting nice so that you trust them and then physically hurting you (or abusing you in another way).

Sometimes people do say nasty things to each other during arguments, but most people apologise and it won't happen often (once a week or more frequently would probably be considered often) - they will take proactive steps to reduce this kind of behaviour. An abuser might not apologise or if they did, they would still repeat their abusive behaviour over and over again. They may tell you that they are going to change but they won't make any effort to do so. This is abuse. Having an argument occasionally where both people sincerely apologise and make an effort to not repeat the argument or similar behaviour is not abuse. This is because from time to time many people do say things during arguments that they don't mean, and they don't think before they say them. An abuser does not care about you and they may sometimes pretend to or act as if they care. Abusers often take pleasure in making you suffer.

Abuse frequency can fluctuate (sometimes this is a tactic to confuse you). It may be helpful to note down when you feel they are being abusive. You can then look back on these notes to see if there are any patterns in their behaviour.

Physical - This is when a person deliberately hits, kicks or physically attacks you in any way.

Professionals should not have sexual/romantic relationships with clients unless it is a professional service they offer

Some professionals such as sex workers or sex surrogates may clearly outline the sexual or relationship services they offer. As a client it is important to remember that they are just services and these kinds of professionals will not love you.

Other professionals who do not offer sex or relationship services to clients would be wrong to have sex or a romantic relationship with a client or former client. The type of professional does not matter. This is because as the professional they have more power than you do; as a client you should be able to access their services with safety and without fear. In addition, the information you share with a professional should not be used to hurt you or manipulate/control you.

Many professions such as teaching and counselling require professionals to be on their register e.g. the BACP (British Association for Counselling and Psychotherapists). To do this, professionals must have a certain level of training and agree to abide by their ethical framework rules. You can report any misconduct or inappropriate behaviour (any sexual or romantic relationship is inappropriate) to their professional body (organisation such as the BACP). If you are unsure, the Citizen's Advice Bureau may be a good source of information. Your local council will also have a Safeguarding Adults team who may also be able to help. Do not feel guilty for reporting misconduct. It is not right for a professional to behave in this way and they may be causing you and others harm.

Common experiences for people experiencing abuse

Abusers choose their words carefully to have maximum impact in hurting your feelings, and controlling you to ensure that you stay with them. Below are some things abusers often say or ways victims of abuse often feel:

1. Abusers make you feel like abuse is your fault or you deserve it.

Often abusers will make you feel like abuse is your fault regardless of the kind of abuse. Each person has to take control of his or her actions, even if you feel you did something wrong in the first place, the person abusing you has the choice to behave like a rational, respectful adult or be an abuser, just as you do.

If an abuser has caused serious harm (i.e. requiring hospital treatment or endangered life) and justifies it as an "accident" and this has happened more than once it is highly unlikely that it was an accident and you are most likely being abused.

Some abusers justify their behaviour by saying you needed to learn a lesson or you need to change in some way. It is not their job to force you to change or behave in a certain way. You are an adult, you can make your own choices and you should be listened to (there are some circumstances, such as if you are sectioned under the Mental Health Act, where other people will make choices on your behalf but those people would be professionals - if professionals are abusing you then you should complain).

2. Abusers want you to keep things a secret.

Commonly abusers will tell you or ask you not to tell anyone about something which has happened. This can also be a sign that you are being abused.

People on the spectrum often feel unsafe and scared to break rules. If you feel you cannot tell someone because you are frightened to break a rule, what about writing a letter or an e-mail to someone who can help you? Writing it in the third person may be a helpful way to communicate what you are trying to say.

Do find a way to communicate, as this rule needs to be broken. Tell someone unconnected to the abuser (either by friendship, work or related to them); someone they do not know or do not speak to.

3. Abusers may try to isolate you.

An abuser may try to limit how often you see your friends and family and want to know what you said to them or what they said to you. They may suggest moving away from people you know, or restricting your telephone access. You are always entitled to keep in contact with your friends and family. If you find someone is trying to isolate you this could be a sign of abuse. There may be some circumstances in which you feel particular people in your life could be a bad influence. If this happens and you are not sure

Useful contacts

Police - in London
- http://content.met.police.uk
- Call 101 for non-emergencies or 999 in emergencies (if you feel your, or someone else's, life may be at risk)

Police - rest of UK (not London)
- www.police.uk
- Call 101 for non-emergencies or 999 in emergencies (if you feel your or someone else's life may be at risk)

Women's Aid (all of the UK)
- www.womensaid.org.uk
- Call 0800 200 0247

whether your concerns are genuine, ask someone who is not connected that those people what they think. Sometimes talking things through can be helpful.

4. You may feel confused about if something would be considered abuse or not.

If you think you have experienced any kind of abuse but you are not sure, you could do one of the following (see useful contacts box on the previous page):

- Call the police - the police have a non-emergency number. Sometimes just talking about the incident(s) can help you think about it in a more clear way. You can also find definitions of terms such as rape and domestic violence on the police's website.
- Call Women's Aid for more information.
- Check with someone you trust who is not friends with or related to the person you feel may be abusing you.

5. Abusers may threaten to leave you.

Abusers may threaten to leave you if you do not do what they want or if you do not put up with their abusive behaviour. You do not deserve to be abused and you can live a life free of abuse. If they do leave you, you will survive and be better off without being abused.

6. Abusers may make you feel like you cannot cope without them.

A lot of people on the autistic spectrum can live independently. However, if you feel this is not possible for you then the support you receive should never be abusive. Abuse potentially increases your support needs, due to the impact the abuse may be having on your mental and physical health.

There is help out there, and many women and men have left abusive situations and succeed in living independently, as I have.

Accessing support through adult social services.

In terms of accessing support because you have experienced abuse, you may be FACS (Fair Access to Care Services) eligible.

This means you may be able to receive money from social services to pay for support, or they may provide support. You can argue for an autism specialist support service, and they do exist around the country.

You are a worthwhile human being who deserves the right support.

This link provides information on FACS: http://www.scie.org.uk/publications/guides/guide33/files/guide33.pdf

7. You are not better off staying with an abuser.

Often abuse can get worse over time and have a huge impact on a person's psychological and physical health. If you leave an abusive situation, this will mean that no more damage will be done to you and you can heal from the abuse you have experienced. But if you stay it gives the abuser the opportunity to continue hurting you.

8. Abusers are not likely to stop abusing you.

Abusers do not usually stop abusing people. They may have periods of time where they are nice and then other times when they are abusive but this is usually done to confuse you so that you will stay.

9. People will believe you.

A lot of people worry that nobody will believe them when they tell people they have been abused. People will believe you, there may be some that don't, but many more will.

10. There are people who will love you and be your friend without abusing you

There are now dating websites and agencies for people on the autistic spectrum and other disabilities (see box).

> **Box 4:**
> **Dating links**
>
> • www.aspieaffection.com
> • www.starsinthesky.co.uk

There are also specialist dating agencies that provide their service for people with and without disabilities. There are many people on the autistic spectrum who have successful loving relationships with non-autistic people.

Everybody is worthy of love. Love and abuse can't go together; because why would you hurt someone you love. Abuse does not help anyone.

If you would be interested in meeting other women who have also experienced abuse, there may be organisations in your area that run support groups. Some women find this beneficial because it makes them feel less alone.

Leaving an abusive situation

People leaving abuse will often go back to the abuser several times before they manage to leave forever. For people who support or care about someone going through this it can be hard to understand why the person would go back to an abuser, but leaving abuse can seem like climbing a huge mountain full of new obstacles.

When you leave an abuser it is important to have no contact with him or her or anyone who is connected to them, such as mutual friends or family members. The abuser could use this contact to control you, encourage you to go back to them or hurt you further.

Friends and professionals often put a lot of emphasis on a person leaving a situation, which is the right thing to do as nobody deserves to be abused. However, having had some experience of this, I can report that the abuser often infiltrates and controls your life in many ways, and this creates dependency meaning you have to start over.

Perhaps a helpful comparison may be the support someone receives after going blind or losing a limb. The dependency you have on your abuser may mean that you would potentially need some mid- to long-term support to help you adjust to life, just like someone who has lost their sight or a limb. For many people leaving an abuser or an abusive home, whilst there is some support, more practical support with dealing with everyday life is often very important. Having a daily structured timetable can be very helpful for people on the spectrum. If you are planning on leaving an abuser, writing a daily timetable for when you leave may be a helpful way to start thinking about your life without the person who has been abusing you.

What it means to take ownership of your life after abuse

Taking ownership of your life after abuse means deciding to deal with problems yourself and, where possible, not depending on others but doing things yourself.

Accepting help is ok too, but when you are able to do something for yourself safely it is important that you try to do so independently.

It can be hard to take ownership of your problems: you may feel very anxious about making decisions and choices. However, the more decisions and choices you make, the more confident you will be. It may be helpful to write a diary of decisions and choices you make during a day: what went well and what did not. This is an exercise similar to something you might do in CBT (Cognitive Behavioural Therapy) and allows you to analyse decisions and choices you have made. By doing this, you can decide what you could do differently next time (if anything) to get a different or better outcome.

You could store this information in alphabetical order by situation for example shopping at a supermarket would go under 'S'. You could write this information down on a computer or on index cards.

Perhaps asking yourself what you could do to solve a particular problem and planning out potential consequences (you could ask a social worker, psychologist or friend to help you with this) in a spider/flow diagram may also be helpful.

How I took ownership of a problem to overcome it

I experienced depression, which was likely to have been triggered by what was happening around me. I tried medication, art therapy etc. I didn't really start to make massive improvements until I took ownership of my problem and designed my own behaviour plan. I had medical supervision from my doctor and I made a set of behavioural goals based around mood mapping (the Liz Miller model as described in "Practical Mood Mapping").

What is mood mapping?

Mood mapping is a way to pictorially represent your emotions.

Dr. Liz Miller suggests doing 4 mood maps a day. My daily behaviour goal was to have 3 mood maps that were in the middle or above (meaning I was neither depressed nor anxious). For doing this I earned an After Eight mint. If I achieved my goal every day for a week then I could have a reward such as going to the cinema; a whole month equated to a larger reward.

I also had to go to the gym 5 times a week and complete an exercise routine. For me this replaced medication. It is important that you do not alter your medication without medical advice and supervision as this could result in side effects and damage your body.

I developed the above plan and was disciplined with myself; I didn't expect a doctor or social worker to tell me what to do, or when to do it.

I have maintained good mental health since this experience, however, like many people on the spectrum I experience very low moods as well as high moods. If you don't experience mood in this way that's OK too. You should discuss this with your doctor.

A way to think about anxiety

Anxiety is a bit like diarrhoea. It's horrible, but you just have to sit through it and it will stop! Anxiety after any kind of abuse is understandable, particularly if you are on the autistic spectrum as it could be difficult to understand people's intentions; this is often due to difficulties with theory of mind.

Theory of mind

Theory of mind is a term used to describe the skill of understanding another person's perspective and intentions.

Theory of mind is one of the skills you would use when watching a film to understand why people behave in particular ways.

Obsession and attachment

Many people on the autistic spectrum become obsessed with, or attached to a person. Sometimes this means you may focus in on that person as if they will be your only friend in the whole world; this can be overwhelming for the other person.

Also if you consider the different relationships you have had in your life (both romantic and platonic), it is likely that you have had friends come and go out of your life.

Contacting people too much

It is vital you do not contact a person too often. You can set rules for yourself such as only sending a message if you have received a reply to a previous message (if you have started a conversation with a person) with the exception that if it is an emergency the rule does not apply.

You do not have to have more than one friend but in order to maintain your friendship you must understand that your friend(s) may have other friends as well as you, and they may not want to spend all their time with you. This is not because they don't like you but they may feel strongly that they like to have many different friends, just like you feel strongly that you only want one friend.

Understanding trust

Trust is something which is built up over time. Abusers often take advantage of trust. You learn to trust them and think that you understand their behaviour, but they may start behaving in an abusive way before going back to being nice and predictable. Or a person works hard to gain your trust and then uses this to control you.

If you decide to make new friends and/or romantic relationships, ensure when you share information about yourself that the other person is sharing the same level of information, in terms of how vulnerable the information can make a person. For example, sharing information about your sexuality makes you more vulnerable than sharing your favourite colour, because if you don't know whether the person will be tolerant with your sexuality, this could make you vulnerable to bullying, teasing or prejudice. If you are unsure what information would make you vulnerable, ask a close friend, social worker or therapist.

In conversation, share information on similar topics and at similar levels of detail as the person with whom you are speaking.

Self-confidence/esteem and building practical strategies

Abuse can reduce self confidence a great deal. Being on the autistic spectrum may mean you are more likely to take things literally and believe what people tell you. So, if an abuser tells you every day that you are ugly or useless, you may believe it.

Upon leaving an abusive situation you have to learn to overcome the way you have learnt to think about yourself. Below are some suggestions. They probably won't all work for you (everyone is different), but the range should mean you will find at least one which will work for you:

1. Use your special interests.

A lot of people on the autistic spectrum have particular topics that they are interested in, and are able to focus on them in a way that most non-autistic people cannot. This can be used in 4 ways:

(1) To comfort: thinking about your special interests in times of anxiety can be helpful. Dr Tony Attwood describes using special interests as "thought blockers". Some people find it useful to have a designated thought pre-prepared; for example, solving maths puzzles, or listing as many fashion designers as they can for each letter of the alphabet etc.

(2) As a reward: for meeting particular targets. These could be behaviour targets or emotional ones equating to allowing yourself to do something, such as watch your favourite film etc.

(3) To gain self worth: if, for example, your interest was theatre, you could volunteer with a local amateur dramatic society. This may help you to feel you have a contribution in the world to make and you would receive gratification from successful performances.

(4) For employment: having a job can have a great benefit to your mental health (providing the environment is right and you have supportive work colleagues). In some parts of the country there are schemes for disabled people to help them access work, such as Project Search. More information can be found at http://odi.dwp.gov.uk/odi-projects/jobs-for-people-with-learning-disabilities/project-search.php. You could also investigate Access to Work, which can be very helpful, even if it can sometimes feel bureaucratic.

2. Do things you enjoy to take care of yourself.

This may seem obvious but many people who have experienced abuse often start to neglect themselves and may feel that they are not important. Doing simple things that give you pleasure and help you stay fit and well can increase feelings of self-worth. This can increase your self-confidence. Types of things that you might do to take care of yourself might be painting your nails, having a bubble bath, going for a run/jog/swim, taking a creative writing course, keeping a diary etc. It depends on the person as to which activity equals taking care of yourself.

3. Create a visual representation of self-confidence.

When I was doing research for my book, I spoke to Dr Tony Attwood. He explained (and I agree) that for some people on the spectrum it is important to ask for praise from people around them. I suggested a visual way of representing this could be to think of self-confidence like a flower. Every time you receive a compliment/praise this is like the flower being watered and growing a bit. You could make this visual: you could write your name, use a photograph of your face or use something pictorial that represents you in a flower head shape. Every time someone compliments you, you could write this on a rectangular piece of paper and stick these pieces of paper onto the flower head to form the stalk. In time, the stalk will grow longer, hopefully along with your self confidence (see diagram).

4. Find success in small steps.

Just because someone else finds a particular task easy such as going to a shop, stepping out the front door or accepting a hug from someone, it doesn't mean you will. Many people on the autistic spectrum and people who have experienced abuse find simple everyday tasks overwhelming. Sometimes splitting a task down into small steps and writing down when you succeed can be very motivating and feel more manageable.

5. List down successes/achievements you have had in the past.

A bit like a personal CV, your achievements

should not be measured against anybody else, because something which is hard to one person may be easy to another. For example, a bus driver driving his or her usual route which they have driven for 20 years is not as big an achievement as someone who has just learnt to drive for the first time. For me, going to the USA for the first time was a huge challenge, but someone else could find going to a supermarket just as big a challenge. Some questions you could ask yourself to help you think about this could be: "What do I do on a daily/weekly/monthly basis that I used to find difficult but can now do?" or "What can I do that I have improved at?"

Setting your own rules - what is OK and what is not OK to you?

Once you are out of an abusive situation, it is important to set your own rules about how you want others to treat you and how you treat yourself.

What kind of behaviour will you accept from friends, romantic partners etc.?

It may help you to write types of behaviours out on post-it notes (or similar) and then sort them into acceptable and unacceptable behaviours. Below are some suggestions of types of behaviours you may list:

- calling me names that make me unhappy
- not changing their behaviour when I ask them to stop behaving in a particular way
- giving me gifts
- asking to borrow money or other belongings off me
- denying me access or controlling me
- hitting me
- flirting with me
- enjoying my special interests

End of chapter thoughts

Please have hope and respect yourself. You are a human being, you are a useful member of society and you are worthy of love.

Top 10 things to remember from this chapter

This is a suggested list, but you could write your own.

1. Many people have left abusive situations and survived and succeeded in life without their abuser. YOU CAN TOO!

2. There are many different types of sexuality and gender, including asexuality, straight, gay, lesbian, gender queer, queer and transgender. It is ok to be any of these sexualities.

3. Abusers choose their words and actions carefully to cause maximum harm to you. They may act nice sometimes but this is to confuse you and make you stay so they can continue to abuse you. They enjoy seeing your pain.

4. Take ownership of your problems. Look for ways/resources to help you overcome them. Abusers often make you feel dependent on them so you will stay longer.

5. As a person on the autistic spectrum you are more likely to stick to rules and believe what you are told. If you think something is wrong, ask the police for help or someone unconnected to the abuser (i.e. not the abuser's friends or family).

6. When leaving an abusive situation, having a structured hour-by-hour timetable may be a helpful way of helping you cope without your abuser.

7. Trust is something built up over time. When you first meet someone, sharing all of your personal problems etc. would make you vulnerable as that person can use it against you. Be mindful of this when starting new relationships with friends or romantic partners - share the same level of information as the person you are talking to.

8. Depicting self-confidence visually may be helpful.

9. Professionals should never have romantic/sexual relationships with clients, unless it is their job (e.g. sex worker).

10. What is a big challenge to one person may not be a big challenge to another person. Achievements are individual. Celebrate the difficulties you work towards overcoming or have overcome.

Chapter 16

Dr Elisabeth Hurley

The Research:
Women and Girls with Autism

Dr Elisabeth Hurley PhD, BSc, has a PhD in Neuroscience, specialising in the development of the body clock. Her academic experience and her interest in autism led her to join Autism West Midlands as Research Officer in October 2012. As Research Officer she ensures that the charity's practice reflects the most recent research and she communicates relevant research in autism to the public.

In April 2013, Elisabeth co-authored a book with Dr Neil Walsh, *The Good and Bad Science of Autism*, which aims to give a brief and easy to read introduction to autism research. She also speaks at conferences on a range of topics including women and girls with autism.

There are on average four times as many men diagnosed with autism than women. This may be because men are more affected by autism or because women are not being recognised and diagnosed. The Extreme Male Brain theory is the most famous theory that addresses this but recent research has shown that the issue may be more complex. Research evidence suggests that there is a gender bias in diagnosis, with women being less likely to be diagnosed compared to men. This may be because women are able to hide their difficulties and learn coping strategies. However, women with autism are also at higher risk of mental health problems so it is important to improve diagnosis so that they can receive support and understanding.

A note on terminology: *the majority of this chapter refers to 'men' and 'women'. However, in some cases, the terms 'boys' and 'girls' are used. This indicates that the research was done in children and not adults. All the information provided here is relevant to both adults and children.*

How many men and women are there diagnosed with autism?

Autism affects around 1.1% of the population[1], with more men diagnosed than women. The current estimates say that there are around four times as many men diagnosed with autism than women, but this depends on who you are counting[2]. In people with autism and learning disabilities, there are only twice as many men diagnosed than women, whereas in people with Asperger syndrome, there are up to 10 or 11 times as many men diagnosed as women[2]. Why are more men diagnosed with autism than women? Is it because autism affects men more than women? Or is it because women are not being recognised and understood?

Although all the studies have found more men diagnosed with autism than women, they do not all agree on *how many* more men there are compared to women. In particular, two recent studies found an average of twice as many men diagnosed compared to women[3,4]. This is different to earlier studies saying that there are on average four times as many men diagnosed as women[2] and implies that there are more women with autism than previously thought. Furthermore, one of the studies looked at the number of boys and girls with autism over time. They found that in younger age groups, there were five times as many boys with autism compared to girls, whereas in older children, there were only twice as many boys with autism compared to girls[3]. This result suggests that there are more girls with autism than previous studies have suggested, but that they are diagnosed later[3].

From its earliest days, there has always been a male bias when describing autism. In his original cases, Kanner described 8 boys and 3 girls. Asperger only described boys and claimed to have never seen a girl with Asperger syndrome in his clinic in Austria and that he saw the first girl with Asperger syndrome in the US in the early 90s[5]. Is there any evidence backing up the claim that autism affects men more than it affects women?

The Extreme Male Brain theory

Probably the most famous theory which addresses this claim is the Extreme Male Brain theory[6]. This theory is an extension of the empathising-systemising theory which says that men are more likely to have a **systemising** brain whereas women are more likely to have an **empathising** brain[6,7]. The researchers can calculate this by asking research participants to complete questionnaires measuring empathising and systemising. Men tend to score higher in the systemising questionnaire whereas women tend to score higher on the empathising questionnaire. When they looked at people with Asperger syndrome or high functioning autism they found that they scored even higher on the systemising questionnaire than men did, suggesting that people with Asperger syndrome or high functioning autism may have an extreme version of the male brain[7].

Empathising can be defined as the ability to identify a person's feelings and respond appropriately. It can be subdivided into cognitive empathy and affective empathy. Cognitive empathy (sometimes referred to as Theory of Mind) can be defined as the drive to identify another's mental state. Affective empathy is the drive to respond to another's mental state with an appropriate emotion. There have been a number of studies which have shown that some people with autism have difficulties with cognitive empathy but have intact affective empathy (Rogers et al., 2007).

Systemising is analysing or building a system which can be mechanical, natural, abstract or collective – for example an interest in trains.

Studies can also try to measure empathising and systemising directly using tasks like trying to guess what a person's emotions are just by looking at their eyes (to measure empathy) or trying to find a simple shape in a more complex figure (to measure systemising). In these studies, researchers have found that women seem to do better at the empathising tasks whereas men seem to do better at the systemising studies. Furthermore, people with Asperger syndrome or high functioning autism seem do worse than men in the empathising studies and do better than men in the systemising studies[8-10]. These results indicate that when looking at empathising and systemising, people with Asperger syndrome or high functioning autism do seem to have an extreme male brain.

The researchers next wanted to know whether or not a person's brain structure would match the extreme male brain theory. Some areas of the brain are bigger in men and some are bigger in women. The researchers looked at areas which are related to empathising and systemising and found that areas which are typically largest in women and smaller in men were even smaller in people with Asperger syndrome or high functioning autism. Similarly, areas which were typically smallest in women and larger in men were even larger in people with Asperger syndrome or high functioning autism[6,11]. So the researchers found that brain structure also followed an extreme male pattern.

Finally, the researchers wanted to know how this came about - why do people with Asperger syndrome or high functioning autism show an extreme form of the male brain? The researchers suggested that foetal testosterone might be involved. Whether a person is a man or a woman is determined by their sex chromosomes. Women have two X chromosomes and men have an X chromosome and a Y chromosome. On the Y chromosome there is a gene called SRY. Activation of this gene triggers the development of testes. These then produce testosterone which takes over the role of masculinisation (making male traits). It is important to note that women also produce testosterone, but much less of it and in a less concentrated form. The idea is that higher levels of testosterone during development result in more masculinisation (male traits). There are a few ways of measuring this and when researchers did this they found indications that women may have been exposed to the lowest levels of testosterone during development, men may have beene exposed to higher levels and people with Asperger syndrome or high functioning autism may have been exposed to the highest levels[12-15].

The research outlined here forms the basis for the Extreme Male Brain theory. However it is important to note that these original studies did not separate out the men and women with Asperger syndrome or high functioning autism. This means that it would not have been possible to say whether or not there are differences between men and women with autism. Furthermore, there were always significantly more men than women in the Asperger syndrome or high functioning autism group, meaning that the results would likely have given a male picture of autism. The researchers did run further studies looking specifically at whether or not there were differences between men and women with Asperger syndrome or high functioning autism in empathising and systemising, as well as the AQ (Autism Spectrum Quotient, which measures autistic traits) and did not show any differences[16-20]. However, most of these studies again used more men than women in the Asperger syndrome or high functioning autism samples. Interestingly, in one of the few studies where they compared equal numbers of men and women with Asperger syndrome and high functioning autism, despite finding no differences in empathising or systemising, they did find that women scored higher than men on the AQ, which means they were reporting more autistic traits than men. What made this finding even more interesting was when they looked at communication skills using the ADOS, a tool which is sometimes used to diagnose autism, they found that women were better at communicating than men. So this study found that although women were better at communicating than men, they also reported more autistic traits. This implies that their communication skills may mean that some women are not identified as having autism, even though they may report more autistic traits[21]. This interesting result demonstrates how useful it is to look at the same number of men and women with Asperger syndrome or high functioning autism: a result that may have been missed if less women had been used gives an interesting insight into why women may not be being diagnosed.

It is not just studies looking at the extreme male brain theory that use more men than women in their Asperger syndrome or high functioning autism groups. Many other areas in autism research also use more men than women. For example, studies looking at brain volume use around eight times as many men as women[22] and studies looking at brain activation while a person does tasks use around fifteen times as many men as women[23]. This means that research often produces a male picture of autism and therefore we do not understand enough about women with autism.

Are there differences between men and women with autism?

There are studies that, instead of looking at why there might be more men than women with autism, look instead at how men and women with autism are different. Studies looking at head circumference suggest that boys with autism have larger heads than the neurotypical population, whereas girls with autism have smaller heads than the neurotypical population[24]. Studies looking at brain structure have also shown differences between men and women with autism. Men with autism seem to have brains that look like neurotypical women's whereas women with autism seem to have brains that look like neurotypical men's[25]. In this study, the researchers suggested that only women with autism may have an extreme male brain whereas men may have a more feminised brain. This finding is different to what was found in other studies on brain structure and the extreme male brain and suggests that changes in brain structure may be more complicated than researchers initially thought. Indeed, it is more likely that brain structure in autism is much more complex than 'male-like' or 'female-like' and that much more research is needed to understand the differences in brain structure, what they mean and how they happen. Other studies have found differences between men and women when looking at how the brain develops[24,26,27], genetic profile[28,29] and markers found in the blood[30]. These studies which show differences between men and women with autism demonstrate that it is indeed important to study both men and women with autism to get a full picture of how autism presents.

Are there any biological reasons why more men might be affected by autism than women?

There is some research which suggests that men may be more susceptible to autism than women. Studies looking at genetics have found that women may be protected from autism risk. These studies found that although men and women showed the same number of autism susceptibility genes, men showed a higher severity of autism than women[31,32]. These studies suggest that somehow, women may be less affected by autism susceptibility genes and may need to have more susceptibility genes to show signs of autism. These results still need to be replicated and there needs to be more research looking at how and why this is happening. However, they do seem to show that there may be a biological reason why women may not be affected by autism as much as men.

Women are being underdiagnosed.

Although there may be a biological reason why women may not be affected by autism as much as men, at present, many women with autism are undiagnosed. There are a number of reasons why this is happening. As mentioned earlier, there has always been a male bias when describing autism[5]. However, although Kanner described 8 boys and 3 girls, he also noted differences between the boys and the girls, suggesting that autism may be expressed differently in girls[5]. Despite this observation, all subsequent descriptions of autism have been based on a male picture of autism. This means that if autism is indeed expressed differently in women, women may not be identified as having autism. Furthermore, the classic diagnostic tools used to diagnose autism are all designed around a male picture of autism and it is well known that these tools are at present not suitable for diagnosing women[33,34]. One diagnostic tool, the ASSQ-REV, was revised to try and include more markers which would be suitable for girls. However, they found that even with these markers, the tool was still not suitable for diagnosing girls. The researchers highlighted that some of the questions asked would be answered differently by boys and girls and could lead to girls not being diagnosed. For example, one question looked at whether the child had a best friend. The researchers found that 70% of boys would say that they didn't have a best friend, whereas only 30% of girls would say this. Therefore, the girl that has a best friend may not be considered to have many social difficulties and may miss out on a diagnosis[33]. Of course, a child is not diagnosed based on one question, but their study highlighted a number of areas where boys and girls answered the questions differently, which could lead to girls missing out on diagnosis.

Studies looking at diagnosis in clinics have shown a clear gender bias in diagnosis[35-38]. In a study where the researchers started off by looking at autistic traits, then looked at who was diagnosed later, they found that even when men and women are matched for severity of autism, it is more likely that the man will be diagnosed with autism than the woman[37]. This happens most often in people with Asperger syndrome and may explain why there are currently 10 times as many men diagnosed with Asperger syndrome compared to women[35,38]. The reasons for this gender bias in diagnosis include, as mentioned above, the fact that the diagnostic tests and descriptions of autism are all based on a male picture of autism, but may also be due in part to the extreme male brain theory which in some cases has been misinterpreted to mean that women cannot have autism.

Diagnostic manuals, which provide guidance on how to diagnose autism, have not addressed the differences between men and women with autism in the past. However, the DSM-5 (the diagnostic manual written by the American Psychiatric Association which is sometimes used in the UK), which was released in May 2013, brings up this issue. The DSM-5 includes the following sentence:

"In clinic samples females tend to be more likely to show accompanying intellectual disability, which suggests that girls without accompanying disability or language delays may go unrecognised, perhaps because of subtler manifestations of social and communication difficulties." [39]

Although this is not a description of autism in women, it is a good start as it specifically says that women with autism may be being undiagnosed because they may not have as many social or communication difficulties, or they can hide them better. It is a call for more research on women with autism so that recognition and diagnosis can be improved.

Why are women being missed?

Although there is not much research on how autism is expressed differently in women, there are a few studies which address this. A recent study looked at emotion recognition. People with autism do not tend to be able to identify emotions as well as the neurotypical population. This study looked at 3,666 children and identified children with autistic-like communication difficulties (133 boys and 88 girls). They wanted to know how good they were at identifying emotions on faces. They found that boys with autistic-like communication difficulties were not able to identify the emotions as often as girls with autistic-like communication difficulties or the neurotypical population (the girls with autistic-like communication difficulties performed almost as well as the neurotypical population). This result suggests that girls with autistic-like communication difficulties are able to identify emotions. However, the researchers then used a second task, which involved identifying emotions using interactions between a triangle and a circle. This task takes away the human element of emotion recognition and uses only social cues to identify the emotions. In this task, neurotypical children were correctly able to identify the emotions. However, neither boys nor girls with autistic-like communication difficulties were able to identify the emotions. This result suggests that although girls with autistic-like communication difficulties may be able to identify emotions when they are on faces, they still have difficulty identifying them when no faces were involved. This suggests that they have learnt how to identify emotions on faces[40]. This study gives us a clue as to why women with autism may not be being identified. They may be learning coping strategies to hide themselves within the neurotypical population. However, they may still have challenges which may make it difficult for them to cope with the demands of a neurotypical world.

Observation studies have also given some clues as to why women may not be being identified[5]. Girls may find it easier to imitate social actions that they see in other children. Girls may be more aware that they need to be social and so try to participate in games, although they rarely initiate games themselves. One reason why girls may know they need to be social is that from birth, we interact with babies in a gender biased way. This happens whether or not we try and avoid dressing babies in pink or blue. So girls are brought up to be more social and therefore know that this is how they should behave[36]. In primary school, girls with autism tend to be mothered by other girls and may be supported and included by their peers. Because they are included in a group, teachers may not notice that there is a problem. On the other hand, boys with autism are more likely to be bullied, or they may be more disruptive at school making them more noticed[41–43]. Girls tend to have more difficulties in secondary school when girls' relationships with each other become much more complicated. Girls may have one special friend and they may care what their peers think and worry about this[5].

Girls may show differences in how they acquire speech. Girls with autism tend to use new words when they learn them while boys with autism may not. This means they may not be identified as having language delay, which could result in girls not being diagnosed. On top of that, our society expects girls to be chattier than boys. However, girls may not use "meaningless" chatter in social situations, but instead they may say what they think and may not understand the subtleties in social situations (in this way, they are similar to boys)[5].

Girls with autism may be more likely to have a rich and elaborate fantasy world and imaginary friends than boys. However, there may not be much shared activity with peers in this imaginary world. In the same way, when they play with dolls, girls may follow a script and may not be able to predict the consequences of the actions of others[5]. Girls may also show less restricted repetitive and stereotyped patterns of behaviour[44].

Whereas boys with autism tend to have technical hobbies which mean they stand out from their peers, girls' interests may be similar to neurotypical girls' (for example animals, celebrities or classical literature). However, girls with autism may have a more intense interest in these things. Girls may compile books of people's names, colour of hair or facts about celebrities for example[5].

Girls tend to internalise things and camouflage their difficulties[43]. This can result in mental health issues. Indeed, there is evidence that women with autism are more likely to develop mental health problems such as anxiety, depression or obsessive compulsive disorder compared to boys. They may also be more at risk of developing anorexia[5,43]. Therefore it is important that girls are diagnosed so that they can get the appropriate support and understanding.

Although there may be some biological evidence that women may be less affected by autism than men, there is still a lot that needs to be done to ensure that women are identified, diagnosed and supported in a gender appropriate way. Understanding the true numbers of women with autism, how to diagnose them and how autism affects their lives will help us to have a greater understanding of autism in general.

References

1.   Brugha, T. S. *et al.* Estimating the prevalence of Autism Spectrum Conditions in Adults: *Extending the 2007 Adult Psychiatric Morbidity Survey.* (2012).

2.   Fombonne, E. Epidemiological surveys of autism and other pervasive developmental disorders: an update. *Journal of autism and developmental disorders* 33, 365–382 (2003).

3.   Idring, S. *et al.* Autism spectrum disorders in the Stockholm Youth Cohort: design, prevalence and validity. *PloS one* 7, e41280 (2012).

4.   Kim, Y. A. *et al.* Prevalence of Autism Spectrum Disorders in a total population sample. *American Journal of Psychiatry* 168, 904–912 (2011).

5.   Gould, J. & Ashton-Smith, J. Missed diagnosis or misdiagnosis? Girls and women on the autism spectrum. *GAP Journal* 12, 34–41 (2011).

6.   Baron-Cohen, S. Autism: the empathizing-systemizing (E-S) theory. *Annals of the New York Academy of Sciences* 1156, 68–80 (2009).

7.   Goldenfeld, N., Baron-Cohen, S. & Wheelwright, S. Empathizing and systemizing in males, females and autism. *Clinical Neuropsychiatry* 2, 338–345 (2005).

8.   Baron-Cohen, S., O'Riordan, M., Stone, V., Jones, R. & Plaisted, K. Recognition of faux pas by normally developing children and children with Asperger syndrome or high-functioning autism. *Journal of autism and developmental disorders* 29, 407–18 (1999).

9.   Baron-Cohen, S., Jolliffe, T., Mortimore, C. & Robertson, M. Another advanced test of theory of mind: evidence from very high functioning adults with autism or asperger syndrome. *Journal of child psychology and psychiatry, and allied disciplines* 38, 813–22 (1997).

10.   Jolliffe, T. & Baron-Cohen, S. Are people with autism and Asperger syndrome faster than normal on the Embedded Figures Test? *Journal of child psychology and psychiatry, and allied disciplines* 38, 527–34 (1997).

11.   Baron-Cohen, S., Knickmeyer, R. C. & Belmonte, M. K. Sex differences in the brain: implications for explaining autism. *Science* (New York, N.Y.) 310, 819–23 (2005).

12.   Lutchmaya, S., Baron-Cohen, S., Raggatt, P., Knickmeyer, R. & Manning, J. T. 2nd To 4th Digit Ratios, Fetal Testosterone and Estradiol. *Early human development* 77, 23–8 (2004).

13.   Manning, J. T., Baron-Cohen, S., Wheelwright, S. & Sanders, G. The 2nd to 4th digit ratio and autism. *Developmental medicine and child neurology* 43, 160–4 (2001).

14.   Auyeung, B. *et al.* Fetal testosterone and autistic traits. *British journal of psychology* (London, England : 1953) 100, 1–22 (2009).

15.   Auyeung, B., Taylor, K., Hackett, G. & Baron-Cohen, S. Foetal testosterone and autistic traits in 18 to 24-month-old children. *Molecular autism* 1, 11 (2010).

16.   Auyeung, B., Baron-Cohen, S., Wheelwright, S. & Allison, C. The Autism Spectrum Quotient: Children's Version (AQ-Child). *Journal of autism and developmental disorders* 38, 1230–40 (2008).

17.   Auyeung, B. *et al.* The children's Empathy Quotient and Systemizing Quotient: sex differences in typical development and in autism spectrum conditions. *Journal of autism and developmental disorders* 39, 1509–21 (2009).

18.   Baron-Cohen, S., Wheelwright, S., Skinner, R., Martin, J. & Clubley, E. The autism-spectrum quotient (AQ): evidence from Asperger syndrome/high-functioning autism, males and females, scientists and mathematicians. *Journal of autism and developmental disorders* 31, 5–17 (2001).

19.   Baron-Cohen, S., Hoekstra, R. a, Knickmeyer, R. & Wheelwright, S. The Autism-Spectrum Quotient (AQ)--adolescent version. *Journal of autism and developmental disorders* 36, 343–50 (2006).

20.   Wheelwright, S. *et al.* Predicting Autism Spectrum Quotient (AQ) from the Systemizing Quotient-Revised (SQ-R) and Empathy Quotient (EQ). *Brain research* 1079, 47–56 (2006).

21.   Lai, M.-C. *et al.* A behavioral comparison of male and female adults with high functioning autism spectrum conditions. *PloS one* 6, e20835 (2011).

22.   Via, E., Radua, J., Cardoner, N., Happé, F. & Mataix-cols, D. Meta-analysis of Gray Matter Abnormalities in Autism Spectrum Disorder. Should Asperger Disorder be Subsumed Under a Broader Umbrella of Autistic Spectrum Disorder? *Archives of General Psychiatry* 68, 409–418 (2011).

23.   Philip, R. C. *et al.* A systematic review and meta-analysis of the fMRI investigation of autism spectrum disorders. *Neuroscience Biobehavioral Reviews* 36, 901–942 (2012).

24.   Ben-Itzchak, E., Ben-Shachar, S. & Zachor, D. a. Specific Neurological Phenotypes in Autism Spectrum Disorders Are Associated with Sex Representation. Autism research : official journal of the International Society for Autism Research 6, 596–604 (2013).

25.   Lai, M.-C. *et al.* Biological sex affects the neurobiology of autism. *Brain : a journal of neurology* 136, 2799–815 (2013).

26.   Schumann, C. M. *et al.* Longitudinal magnetic resonance imaging study of cortical development through early childhood in autism. *The Journal of neuroscience : the official journal of the Society for Neuroscience* 30, 4419–27 (2010).

27.   Surén, P. *et al.* Early growth patterns in children with autism. *Epidemiology* 24, 660–670 (2013).

28.   Gilman, S., Iossifov, I., Levy, D. & Ronemus, M. Rare de novo variants associated with autism implicate a large functional network of genes involved in formation and function of synapses. *Neuron* 70, 898–907 (2011).

29.   Szatmari, P. *et al.* Sex differences in repetitive stereotyped behaviors in autism: implications for genetic liability. *American Journal of Medical Genetics. Part B, neuropsychiatric genetics: the official publication of the International Society of Psychiatric Genetics.* 159B, 5–12 (2012).

30.   Schwarz, E. *et al.* Sex-specific serum biomarker patterns in adults with Asperger's syndrome. *Molecular psychiatry* 16, 1213–20 (2011).

31.   Hallmayer, J. *et al.* Genetic heritability and shared environmental factors among twin pairs with autism. *Archives of general psychiatry* 68, 1095–102 (2011).

32.   Robinson, E. B., Lichtenstein, P., Anckarsäter, H., Happé, F. & Ronald, A. Examining and interpreting the female protective effect against autistic behavior. *Proceedings of the National Academy of Sciences of the United States of America* 110, 5258–62 (2013).

33.   Kopp, S. & Gillberg, C. The Autism Spectrum Screening Questionnaire (ASSQ)-Revised Extended Version (ASSQ-REV): an instrument for better capturing the autism phenotype in girls? A preliminary study involving 191 clinical cases and community controls. *Research in developmental disabilities* 32, 2875–88 (2011).

34.   Lai, M.-C., Lombardo, M. V, Chakrabarti, B. & Baron-Cohen, S. Subgrouping the autism "spectrum": reflections on DSM-5. *PLoS biology* 11, e1001544 (2013).

35.   Begeer, S. *et al.* Sex differences in the timing of identification among children and adults with autism spectrum disorders. *Journal of autism and developmental disorders* 43, 1151–6 (2013).

36.   Goldman, S. Opinion: Sex, gender and the diagnosis or autism - A biosocial view of the male preponderance. *Research in Autism Spectrum Disorders* 7, 675–679 (2013).

37.   Russell, G., Steer, C. & Golding, J. Social and demographic factors that influence the diagnosis of autistic spectrum disorders. *Social psychiatry and psychiatric epidemiology* 46, 1283–93 (2011).

38.   Shattuck, P. T. *et al.* The timing of identification among children with an autism spectrum disorder: findings from a population-based surveillance study. *Journal of the American Academy of Child and Adolescent Psychiatry* 48, 474–483 (2009).

39.   American Psychiatric Association. *Diagnostic and statistical manual of mental disorders.* (American Psychiatric Association, 2013).

40.   Kothari, R., Skuse, D., Wakefield, J. & Micali, N. Gender Differences in the Relationship Between Social Communication and Emotion Recognition. *Journal of the American Academy of Child & Adolescent Psychiatry* 52, 1148–1157 (2013).

41.   Bölte, S., Duketis, E., Poustka, F. & Holtmann, M. Sex differences in cognitive domains and their clinical correlates in higher-functioning autism spectrum disorders. *Autism : the international journal of research and practice* 15, 497–511 (2011).

42.   Mandy, W. P. L., Charman, T. & Skuse, D. H. Testing the construct validity of proposed criteria for DSM-5 autism spectrum disorder. *Journal of the American Academy of Child and Adolescent Psychiatry* 51, 41–50 (2012).

43.   Solomon, M., Miller, M., Taylor, S. L., Hinshaw, S. P. & Carter, C. S. Autism symptoms and internalizing psychopathology in girls and boys with autism spectrum disorders. *Journal of autism and developmental disorders* 42, 48–59 (2012).

44.   Van Wijngaarden, P. J. *et al.* Gender and Age Differences in the Core Triad of Impairments in Autism Spectrum Disorders: A Systematic Review and Meta-analysis. *Journal of autism and developmental disorders* 44, 627–635 (2014).